FIRE:
THE FURIOUS BURNING LOVE OF OUR BRIDEGROOM

Fasten me upon your heart as a seal of fire forevermore. This living, consuming flame will seal you as my prisoner of love. My passion is stronger than the chains of death and the grave, all consuming as the very flashes of fire from the burning heart of God. Place this fierce, unrelenting fire over your entire being.
Song of Songs 8:6 TPT

Fire:
The Furious Burning Love of Our Bridegroom

By

Paul L Cox

FIRE: THE FURIOUS BURNING LOVE OF OUR BRIDEGROOM

By Paul L Cox

Aslan's Place Publications
13312 Ranchero Rd
STE 18, PMB 522
Oak Hills, CA 92344
aslansplace.com

All Rights Reserved. No part of this book may be reproduced or transmitted in any form or by any means — electronic or mechanical, including photocopying, recording, or by any information storage and retrieval system — without written permission from the authors except as provided by the copyright laws of the United States of America. Unauthorized reproduction is a violation of both federal and spiritual laws.

Unless otherwise indicated, scriptures are taken from the: New King James Version (NKJV): New King James Version®. Copyright © 1982 by Thomas Nelson, Inc., publishers. Used by permission. All rights reserved.

Other Biblical References:

The ESV® Bible (The Holy Bible, English Standard Version®) copyright © 2001 by Crossway Bible, a publishing ministry of Good News Publishers. Used by permission. All rights reserved.

Scripture quotations marked NLT are taken from the *Holy Bible*, New Living Translation, copyright ©1996, 2004, 2015 by Tyndale House Foundation. Used by permission of Tyndale House Publishers, Inc., Carol Stream, Illinois 60188. All rights reserved.

Scripture taken from the HOLY BIBLE, NEW INTERNATIONAL VERSION. Copyright © 1973, 1978,1984, 1985 International Bible Society. Used by permission of Zondervan Bible Publishers.

Copyright 2025, by Paul L Cox

All rights reserved.

Editor: Barbara Kain Parker

Cover Design: Brodie Schmidtke

ISBN: 979-8-2840-9591-1

Printed in the United States of America

TABLE OF CONTENTS

FOREWORD 7

PROPHETIC WORD 9

AUTHOR'S NOTE 10

INTRODUCTION 11

CHAPTER ONE: *AND SO IT BEGINS* 12

CHAPTER TWO: *FUEGO!* 16

CHAPTER THREE: *THE BURNING BUSH* 20

CHAPTER FOUR: *THE BURNING BUSH APPEARS* 25

CHAPTER FIVE: *UNDERSTANDING THE BURNING BUSH* 29

CHAPTER SIX: *EXPECTING THE BURNING BUSH* 32

CHAPTER SEVEN: *ENCOUNTERING THE BURNING BUSH* 38

CHAPTER EIGHT: *BURNING, BURNING, BURNING…* 43

CHAPTER NINE: *THE FURNACE* 48

CHAPTER TEN: *INTRODUCING THE LINEN MAN* 53

CHAPTER ELEVEN: *EXPLORING THE LINEN MAN* 59

CHAPTER TWELVE: *DANIEL AND THE LINEN MAN* 64

CHAPTER THIRTEEN: *DANIEL'S CONCLUSION* 68

CHAPTER FOURTEEN: *THE LITERAL WORD OF GOD* 72

CHAPTER FIFTEEN: *FIRE & THE DAY OF THE LORD* 76

CHAPTER SIXTEEN: *FIRE - BLESSING OR JUDGMENT* 85

CHAPTER SEVENTEEN: *THE SUN OF RIGHTEOUSNESS* 89

CHAPTER EIGHTEEN: *ROOTS AND BRANCHES* 95

CHAPTER NINETEEN: *BRANCHES AS BELIEF SYSTEMS* 112

CHAPTER TWENTY: *A TESTIMONY: ROOTS & BRANCHES – THE BEGINNING* 117

CHAPTER TWENTY-ONE: *FREE AS A CALF* 121

CHAPTER TWENTY-TWO: *THE PLOWMAN* 126

CHAPTER TWENTY-THREE: *THE BRIDEGROOM'S PASSION* ..133

CHAPTER TWENTY-FOUR: *A SUSTAINED BURNING* 138

AFTERWORD 142

APPENDIX ONE: *PROPHETIC WORDS OVER THE YEARS* 144

APPENDIX TWO: *SPIRITUAL SERVANTS OF THE MOST HIGH WHO ARE ON FIRE* 158

Foreword

It would be appropriate to say that Paul L Cox has been my mentor for the past twenty years. When I first walked into Aslan's Place in January 2005, it was with a very limited knowledge of the presence and power of the Holy Spirit, and the idea of exploring the heavenly realms had never even crossed my mind. But after the very first hour of the very first day, I was hooked, and I walked away from those basic introductory sessions knowing that I never wanted to leave this place. I'd found my spiritual family; I'd finally come home.

For the first few years I was like a sponge (still am, for that matter!), soaking up revelatory insights of which I'd never dreamed, experiencing lots of deliverance and eventually completing an internship and becoming a prayer minister. It was my delight to travel with Paul's team to locations throughout the USA as well as to Ireland, England and Canada, with each trip still holding a dear place in my heart.

Little did I know in 2005 that I had boarded a spiritual rocket ship, so to speak, because the revelation poured out like water as months and then years progressed and is still coming like a flood.

I began editing articles for Paul during that first year, some of which became the basis for his book, *Heaven Trek*, published in 2007. He continued writing and published *Sacrifice the Leader* in 2008 and *Come Up Higher* in 2010. New generational prayers also kept being developed at an astounding rate so along came the *Aslan's Place Prayer Manual*, which is now updated every few years because apparently the Lord never tires of giving us new prayers to help set His people free.

Soon after *Come Up Higher* came out, Paul started talking to me about us writing a book together, and we threw the idea around for quite a while. What should we write about? Finally, we spent an afternoon laying out all the possible topics at that time and it soon became clear that this wouldn't fit into just one book, so the *Exploring Heavenly Places* series was born, which grew to include fourteen books with Paul, Rob Gross, Brian Cox and me as the contributing authors. When the Lord impressed Paul that the series was finished, along came *Power Outage* and *Revelation of the Vault* (with Rob) as well as *In the Midst of the Storm: Stillness* and *Light Clothed in Darkness: A Mystery* (with me).

I have been so blessed to co-author a dozen books with Paul and to edit those he's written with Rob Gross.

So now we come to *Fire: The Furious Burning Love of Our Bridegroom*, Paul's first solo book since 2010, which I am honored both to edit and endorse. This book is extra special to me because I've been honored to come alongside of Paul as he endured its heavy cost.

Barbara Kain Parker
Standing in Faith Ministries

Prophetic Word

We Are Entering a Time like Acts

Thus says the Lord, "We are entering a time like Acts. The Acts Church shall arise in the midst of the salaciousness and the sorcery. **The Acts Church shall arise — a fiery people with the fire of the Holy Spirit on their words**," says the Lord. "For I have called and anointed them for this time, where Acts shall happen through the power of the Holy Spirit, and Acts shall be judged as well," says the Lord. "Your acts are being weighed," says the Lord.

Amada Grace

https://www.elijahlist.com/words/display_word.html?ID=32505#word-truncate

Author's Note

When an author writes a book, it is important to understand the scope of the audience that will read the book. Many of us are interested in the Hebrew and Greek words and their meaning and etymology. Others prefer to avoid the academic investigation of all the nuances of language and theology. I had originally thought of placing information about the Hebrew and Greek into an appendix, but my study uncovered a reality I needed to address. It is only by carefully examining the Hebrew and Greek that we can understand the nuances of the language, which finally help us understand what is happening in our lives. We cannot avoid a more in-depth study so that the book becomes a popular easy read.

> *Always be eager to present yourself before God as a perfect and mature minister, without shame, as one who correctly explains the Word of Truth.*
> *2 Timothy 2:15*

INTRODUCTION

It had been unrelenting, unending, annoying and painful; hour after hour, day after day, month after month. Two years passed, and then came an unexpected shift into something unknown, unexpected and even more agonizing. What was this now? Would it ever end? Who could help me understand what was happening to me? Where could I go for answers?

It all began on Pentecost, May 30, 2020, and then shifted on Pentecost, June 5, 2022, finally ending on January 8, 2025, on a Caribbean cruise.

In the midst of all of this, I had a dream in which I was holding a book with the entitled *FIRE*. At the bottom of the book were the words, "Aslan's Place Publications". In the dream I asked, "Who is the author of this book?" Almost two weeks later as I was pondering the dream I had the sudden realization that I was to write this book, **FIRE: THE FURIOUS BURNING LOVE OF OUR BRIDEGROOM**. But how do you write a book on the experiences you've have when you do not fully understand those experiences? Walk with me as I share my journey.

Chapter One:
And So it Begins

The Lord had instructed me to hold a gathering on Pentecost, May 30, 2020. How could this be? The governor of California had outlawed all public gatherings because of covid. I could go to jail for disobeying this directive but choosing to obey the Lord and not the governor, I sent out an invitation for this Saturday meeting. A small group gathered at Aslan's Place in Apple Valley, CA to wait on the Lord with high expectation that the power of God would fall on us. As we surrendered to what the Lord wanted to do a good friend asked if she could stand in front of me. I agreed, not fully comprehending the significance of that moment. Positioning herself directly in front of me, she pointed directly at me and said, "The Lord is going to clean off your DNA." The word hit me with such force that I was thrown back into my chair and immediately I could feel a deliverance begin.

Perhaps some background would be helpful: In 1991, after resigning from the pastorate in a southern California American Baptist church, I sensed an unusual pressure on the top, left side at the back of my head. I inquired of a friend who had begun seeing in the Spirit to investigate what she saw. She conveyed that she was seeing a demon, and a thought occurred to me, "Tell the demon to leave." As instructed, I commanded the demon to leave and the pressure on my head lessened. Over a period of months, I had the same experience of sensing evil, commanding it to leave and feeling the relieving of pressure on my head. The Lord had trained my senses to discern evil.

Sometime later, a new pressure was felt on my head and after inquiring of the Lord, I discerned that I was sensing an angel. He was now showing me how to feel an angel.

Over a period of years (which continues to this day), the Lord would train my senses to discern dozens of spiritual beings, each on a different location on my head and body, until there were so many discernments that I now have multiples on the same site and have to go through my 'mental rolodex' to get His confirmation of what it is.

Sometime around 1997, I answered a call from a friend in North Pole, Alaska, a small community on the outskirts of Fairbanks. The Lord had told him to call me and share a scripture he had received for me:

> *That evening they brought to him many who were oppressed by demons, and he cast out the spirits with a word and healed all who were sick.*[1]

Then he asked, "Do you know what this means to you?" I seemed to have immediate understanding that in my future prayer sessions, I was to speak the word 'leave'. My first attempt startled me. When I said, "Leave," immediately I could feel movement on my 'default evil location' at the top, left, back, side of my head. The Lord was removing a whole system of evil off the person, and I felt different levels of pain as the deliverance continued. At times, the pressure was exceptionally robust and then it would decrease.

After ministering numerous times, I noticed a pattern as I would 'lock into' a person and perceive the varying intensity of the deliverance over a period of three days. Sometimes the pain was excruciating, but little did I know that I was being prepared to experience a much deeper level of pain through my discernment.

My deliverance that was initiated at Aslan's Place on May 30, 2020, did not stop. Month after month, year after year as I tried to lead a normal life with my wife, family and ministry it was always in the background with unrelenting deliverance coming off in wave after wave of oscillating pain. The nights were even worse. Often, I would wake up around midnight with extreme, intensely painful deliverance, often so brutal that I would literally scream into my pillow as the pain crossed the threshold of my ability to contain my cries. Over the months and years, I could name the different evil beings being extricated from me – fallen thrones, elders, rulers and mighty ones, fallen sons, fallen kings, walls, windows, dragons, strongman systems, beast systems, leviathan systems, queen of heaven systems, deep darkness, and zodiac systems. Adding to this misery the Lord began a deliverance on land areas in different parts of the United States which I could also feel. During this period, I was also called to fast many times, which only seemed to add to the torment.

Throughout the course of this deliverance journey, the Lord would reassure me that He was at work in me and that a change would come. I held on to these promises/words:

- June 3, 2020: I'm going to take Paul into the deep beyond the depths ever reached

- July 25, 2020: The reproach shall no longer be upon your heads but a crown of blessing instead

- July 25, 2020: Tell Paul there is a new way of deliverance

- September 10, 2020: Paul, He is taking you out of a season of imbalance, fatigue, tiredness and exhaustion and bringing you into a broad and spacious place. This next season will be a season of teaching and imparting.

There is a shift from the warfare to teaching, training and imparting.

- October 21, 2020: Transition. Transformation. Transportation. You have been shifted into a new dimension of My glory and power

- October 23, 2020: Paul, you are about to walk into something so new and fresh and refreshing! Don't do things as they were; do things as they are!

Then came Pentecost June 5, 2022, and there began a series of events that rocked my world.

---

[1] Matthew 8:16 ESV

Chapter Two:
Fuego!

On June 3, 2022, a friend sent me a personal word from a spiritual scroll:

> This day, this day, all oppression will cease
>
> For the wheels, the wheels, the wheels of power that have tried to steam roll you will cease. No more, for this day I have set my servants in place to release thee from the depths of captivity that thou didst not know of.
>
> The intertwining, the weavings, the interconnected cords of the nations, the DNA that I see and thou dost not.
>
> Free this day, you are free, and I am returning to thee what has been stolen (seeing long strands of DNA removed from the dimensions and restored)

I had no hint as to what it meant. Now I do. Through the word the Lord was preparing me for what would begin happening two days later, June 5, 2022.

The burning was not intense at first. During the night I would briefly feel immense warmth and then burning for a few minutes. Gradually the burning increased to an intensity that would become unbearable. At this point, it would start around midnight and would transition into an inferno on my back. Often, it would feel like rippling waves of flames scorching me until I believed I would not survive the process. I imagined it as a blowtorch oscillating up and down my back. During my journey, I wrote on August 2, 2022:

> For the last few nights (actually, for several weeks), I have awakened with fire burning so strongly that I could barely stand it (tested by fire?). Last evening, I was experiencing more deliverance and during the night felt the golden pipes very strongly. Early this morning in my sleep, I was aware that something was taken out of my brain, perhaps a couple of things. I woke up feeling as if a tumor was taken out.

I tried to communicate to others what was happening, but no one was able to give me any understanding. Because of my discernment I knew deliverance was taking place, but why this method? Was anyone else experiencing this?

How can I describe what was happening to me? In past years I have experienced the power of the Lord. For example, while in Argentina we were invited to walk through a 'fire" tunnel'. I felt the anointing, but it was not like the fire I was experiencing now. Often in Argentina, the anointed leaders would yell out, "Fuego, fuego," and laugh as the power of the Lord would fall on the people. But while that fire was powerful, it was not like I was now experiencing; it was not the crackling fire on my nighttime visitations.

I looked further back in my journal and discovered a word from my friend Rob Gross:

> March 27, 2021: Life is in the river. The door has opened, and the Lord is inviting those who are willing to go deeper into the river. There were waters of refreshing in Toronto and Pensacola and

Lakeland. Those outpourings were just the hors d'oeuvres. In years past, Paul, I called Aslan's Place higher but now I am calling Aslan's Place deeper. This is deeper than the depths; it's the place of revelation and understanding; it's the place where My heart abides. All will be shaken and those who do not make the shift will cast adrift in the flood of My glory and <u>fire</u>. The days ahead are filled with hope, for there are new tools; there are weapons of kingdom destruction that will be made available to the Aslan's Place nation. Let hope arise for the Kingdom is here.

New revelation is in the river. The church's understanding of the apostolic wineskin is about to be turned upside down for the kingdom of God is not a matter of talk but of power. It is an apostolic reformation.

I searched my personal journal again and found another clue, a prophetic word given to me on June 3, 2022, by Dawn Bray.

> The ancient ones are coming
> They are seeking to gain more power
> The ungodly grid is their access point
> Through the byways and paths of mire
> You will know them by discerning
> The false will no longer align
> The vines will reject the branches
> That should not be attached to the vine
>
> The Branch will come and lead the way
> Out of the mire to the ancient path
> Alignment will come, the false will bow

The grid will shift, and I will close the shaft

Come through the gate
Then open (step in) the door
The light of My face will cause you to soar
Into the heights on the ancient paths

No more to roam the byways of lack

I'm going to take Paul into the deep beyond the depths ever reached by divine investment of years and years.

He's learned to trust Me and go beyond fears to dive deep inside in the submarine. Take the scrolls and open them alone with Me in the deep to learn new things, all during sleep. Deeper, deeper, deeper still; revelation from a wheel within a wheel. My glory dwells within the deep, and he will bring it back like the ice and sleet; where up is down and down is up, dimensional shifting will open up the gates and doors not opened till now. Follow Me and I will show you how DNA and RNA hidden in glory are all waiting to align and open their story. "There is healing in my wings," says the Sun of Righteousness but man never knew it would happen like this. One by the bush, two by the bush, three by the bush, four; press in, persevere and I'll tell you more. Pray for Paul to open the gate; the time is now; it's not too late

The bush! It is the burning bush. Was I in the midst of the burning bush?

CHAPTER THREE:
THE BURNING BUSH

The burning bush, documented in Exodus 3, tells the story of Moses, who having fled from Egypt is now forty years older. As an eighty-year-old, he is still out tending the sheep, and his attention is drawn to a peculiar sight in the desert - a bush is on fire but is not consumed by the flames. Moses later described what he saw and revealed that it was the Angel of the Lord appearing as fire. Eventually Moses and the children of Israel would follow this pillar of fire throughout the wilderness. As Moses came close to the bush, the Lord spoke to him; note that it was not the Angel of the Lord but Elohim who spoke. Moses was told that He, Elohim, was the God of Moses' father, Arman, a Levite. He was also informed that Elohim's desire was that Moses would lead His people out of Egypt and into the promise land.

A little background regarding Moses: He had grown up in Egypt after his mother placed him in a basket, which was left in a clump of reeds in the Nile River. This was an attempt to save him from Pharoh's order for all Hebrew boy babies to be thrown into the Nile. Rescued by Pharaoh's daughter, he grew up as a member of the royal household. Historically we are knowledgeable of the pagan ritual practices of the Egyptians, which considered Pharaoh to be a god. Imagine Moses growing up in this environment. He would have worshipped the over 150 different gods of Egypt. We are informed in Acts 7 that the Israelites brought out the tabernacle of Moloch from Egypt, and Moses would have been aware of that tabernacle. He would also have participated in over forty different pagan religious festivals during a calendar year, was exposed to human sacrifice and may have engaged in some of them as part of Pharaoh's household. The depth of evil associated with the Egyptians is still being explored today, but Moses was intimately aware of it and, more than likely, he was a willing participant. All of that was about to change.

Having conducted hundreds of generational prayer sessions I have painfully discerned the depth of evil that exists in the generational line of individuals who have been exposed to the horrors of such evil, especially the wickedness of Satanic Ritual Abuse. I wonder about the scope of corruption that had invaded Moses' spirit and soul because Egypt is counted among the evilest of societies and he lived daily in that environment. But now he had encountered the living God.

Moses found himself in the presence of his creator, speaking directly to I AM. It was the presence of the Radiant Glory of the eternal living God. I now ask, "What would be the effect of such an encounter?" I am now speaking logically and thoughtfully: One cannot be that close to the power of holiness and purity and not be affected physically, emotionally and spiritually. I now surmise that at that moment of encountering I AM, Moses must have entered a deliverance that I believe lasted for a long time, perhaps culminating during the most drastic of fasts ever recorded, a forty day fast of food and **water.** It was this cleansing that allowed the Power of the Almighty to flow through him in such strength that the glory of God was able to penetrate and permeate him to such a level that he is counted among the few who have walked in heightened miracles, signs and wonders. One cannot be so close to the eternal fire of the Holy One of Israel and not be consumed by that fire.

I have my own burning bush story, and fortunately I can recount it accurately because from the very beginning of my journey in deliverance, prayer ministry and discernment I have recorded all the words I have received as well as my experiences with the Lord. The first recorded word about the burning bush was on December 11, 2003, and it would become the roadmap for a journey I did not know I was going to take. Then, during ministry an angel came and said there is generational bondage and that this is a new revelation (note the **bold** words):

> It is demonic, not dissociative.
>
> It is in the dimensions.
>
> You have never been there.
>
> The revelation will not come at once; it will come in pieces.
>
> This is the key you've asked for and are picking up. You've entered the door.
>
> Wait for more doors, wait for more doors.
>
> **Only the fire of God can burn it out. Wait for the fire, wait for the fire!**
>
> Multitudes will come, will come to Aslan's Place.
>
> People will come to be set free.
>
> Holy, holy, holy, holy, holy, holy; holy of holies!
>
> **Remember the burning bush.**
>
> You will see it, you will see it, you will see it.
>
> That's when you'll get your revelation.
>
> **Watch for it, watch for it, the burning bush, the burning bush.**
>
> Shout the trumpets, shout the trumpets.

When it comes, you'll be consumed with everlasting fire, everlasting fire.

There is a purpose for all this, and you will see it.

We're sorry for you, (weeping) but the glory has to be shown, the glory, the glory of God.

We weep for you, (weeping) but the glory will come."

Keep the fire going, keep the fire going, keep the fire going, keep the fire going; never let it go out!

What's coming to Aslan's Place is bigger than anything you can imagine.

You have no idea how big; you have no idea HOW BIG, how big, how big, how big, how big.

The land is yours, is yours. it's yours.

The winds of change are coming, the winds of change are coming, the winds of change are coming!

Blow the trumpet! Blow the trumpet, blow the trumpet, blow the trumpet!

Go round and round and round and round and round and round.

It's yours, it's yours; it's yours, it's yours.

What is your vision? What is your vision? What is your vision?

Multiply it by hundreds, hundreds, hundreds, by thousands, thousands.

It's too small. Get it bigger, bigger. Get it bigger.

I am Gabriel, Gabriel announcing the new birth, new birth.

New revelation, new revelation.

Shout the trumpet, shout the trumpet.

March, march! March across the land, march across the land.

You will see the berries, you will see the berries, you will see the berries.

When you see the berries watch out! Watch for the berries.

They will be a sign; they will be a sign.

Watch for the berries where there are no berries.

They will be a sign.

There will be growth; there will be growth.

This is your sign."

No glory can be taken from Me for I am holy.

You are lifted up because of My, of My, of My righteousness.

My glory is coming.

It will fill this place.

When I come no one will stand.

Get going, get going

I had my orders. I was to watch for the burning bush.

Chapter Four:
The Burning Bush Appears

It was a typical warm day in Hesperia, CA on Sunday, August 17, 2005. We had finished week one of an Aslan's Place School of Discernment and preparations were being made for our Advanced School during the second week. The day had begun with a cloudless sky, but by early afternoon a single cloud had formed over the high desert. Within a couple of hours, the entire, vast desert sky had transformed into what appeared to be a single, huge thunderstorm. My estimate was that the sky was filled with this black cloud for over 30 miles. By sundown, massive cloud-to-cloud lightning and cloud-to-ground lightning strikes penetrated the atmosphere. Heavy rain and hail blasted the desert and flash flooding occurred in low areas. As I sat in the Aslan's Place Victorian house, which was both our home and ministry center, I watched with concern as the lightning came closer and closer to us. I ran to the back house to unplug the computer server but was too late. Lightning hit the building and blew out the server.

Following the second day of our advanced school on Tuesday, a friend came into the house and stated that I needed to come with her to see something that I would not believe. I was very resistant because of fatigue and suggested that I could live without seeing that, but she was very insistent. Rather than walk, she drove me only a few houses west of the Victorian and we walked to the back of a house on an ally. I looked down and there was a small bush on fire. How could that be? So much rain had fallen that another house owned by Aslan's Place on the east side of the Victorian had seriously flooded. Another nearby location in the desert had received eighteen inches of rain.

It was now two days after that historic storm. The next day, Wednesday, our friend returned to the burning bush, and it was still burning. She transferred the bush onto an oven pan and brought it into the seminar room. As we all looked at the bush, it disintegrated into a pile of ash and smoke filled the room. I asked, "What kind of bush is this?" It was a sagebrush. Little did we know that about 7 years later, after much searching for a new location, Aslan's Place would move into a property on Sagebrush Street in Apple Valley.

The Lord began to speak:

> I AM Power; here to deliver the fullness of God's promise to you, Paul. Four corners of the world - you are going to go to the four corners of the world, to the seven Seas. There is another well to be dug. Find it.

> You are looking for an ordinary house but is not an ordinary house. It's an unusual house, an unusual land (this is the current Sagebrush property in Apple Valley).

> Enter into the Holy of Holies.

> You will find another key in the Holy of Holies; you will find another key in the Holy of Holies.

> That is the key to the front door; that is the key to the front door.

> There will be another burning bush; there will be another burning bush.

> And another one; and another one.
>
> You are moving; you are moving. Get Moving; get moving; get moving.
>
> I am Promise. I am here to deliver the fullness of God's Promise to you, Paul.
>
> Four corners of the world. To the seven seas.
>
> There's another well to be dug. Find the well.
>
> You are looking for an ordinary house. It's not an ordinary house. You'll find another key in the Holy of Holies. There'll be another burning bush; there'll be another burning bush, and another one.

In the Lord's mercy and in preparation for what is to come, He communicates to us what to expect in the future. The wonder of all of this is you can hear the words but not fathom the concepts being shared. It is like Zechariah who, seeing in a vision the olive trees and the golden pipes, was addressed by the angel, "Do you not know what this is?" Unfortunately, we are often oblivious to what we are seeing and hearing. But we do not remain unknowing because eventually the word is fulfilled, and clarity comes. The following word from Jana Green on March 1, 2017, exemplifies this:

> When you encounter I AM, you will encounter eternal peace and lasting power. I AM is the origin; I AM is the center of who God is and where creation began - it is the center of His throne. Everything we need is in I AM; We don't need anything in I AM. It is the eternal gate, the sum of all things, the reality of everything, the place of original design. You must enter in to be aligned and refined to your

original design. El Shaddai is in the center of I Am. Mount Zion is there too.

The message had been delivered but was not fulfilled until 6 ½ years later, on November 11, 2023. Only then did I understand.

I Am was first experienced by Moses at the burning bush, and now I would too.

Chapter Five:
Understanding the Burning Bush

There often is a pattern in the delivery of prophetic words. There is great excitement when a spiritual being is discerned, and the message is given; great hope is experienced, and expectation accelerates. But the physical reality sets in and one wonders about the authenticity of the word. The Lord is not silent about this process:

> ...*he had sent a man ahead of them, Joseph, who was sold as a slave. His feet were hurt with fetters; his neck was put in a collar of iron; until what he had said came to pass, the word of the* LORD *tested him.*[1]

Joseph had received prophetic promises through a dream from Yahweh but then endured hardship and affliction along with the word. The promises of the word tested him until it they came to pass. The Hebrew word for 'test' is *ṣārap* and is translated *sme*lt, refine, test. (ASV and RSV sometimes identical, others varied; both also "goldsmith," "refine," "try"; ASV also "founder," "purge"; RSV also "silversmith," "cast," "smelt," "prove true.")[2]

The implication is clear - one is tested by fire and the words I'd received about the burning bush, and I AM was going to test me.

It was now 2023: Donna and I had just experienced a glorious time in Oahu, Hawaii. It is always a joy to minister with Rob Gross in Aiea, Hawaii at Mountain View

Community Church. The fellowship in Aiea is so very open to any new move of the Lord and each day is filled with wonder. The Lord had established the Kingdom Institute at the warehouse building God had provided for MVCC.[3] But where was the interest? Upon returning to the high desert, I shared with Rob that there seemed no way forward for me. The Victorian house in Hesperia, CA had been sold, and the funds invested in a condo in Kaneohe, HI, about 20 minutes from the church. Donna and I would live while ministering in HI. The church itself was amazing but interest from those outside of it was close to non-existent. Now what? How could we justify the expense of the condo, a car and the travel back and forth if the Institute wasn't thriving?

We'd also returned home to chaos. Our daughter, Christy, had been undergoing cancer treatment for several years and had decided that she could no longer work for Aslan's Place and began fulltime disability. She had been our office manager since 1999. Now, her final report to us was that the bank account for Aslan's Place was critically low. Donna and I realized we were at a crisis point and without intervention by the Lord we would need to sell the condo in Hawaii, perhaps also the Sagebrush property, and would have to reimagine what Aslan's Place would look like in the future. This decision did not seem reasonable to us, and nothing made sense. The Lord had spoken to us hundreds of times about what He is going to do in Hawaii and at Aslan's Place, but the reality was there were current financial needs, and we decided to make a firm decision on June 1, 2023.

On May 17, 2023, I had a dream. I was in a bus driving a group up to the mountain where the fire of God fell after Elijah prayed. We were waiting for the new fire to fall, but I realized that I had left and started going back down the mountain in a car before the fire fell. I arrived at an exit and attempted to turn around in a parking lot but hit one car, which then hit several other cars. As I awoke, I understood the dream.

The interpretation: In the dream, I was at Mountain View Community Church in Aiea, Hawaii. It was important that I not leave too soon, or I would miss the fire of God falling and my decision could negatively affect other ministries.

The next day a prophetic friend texted, "I feel to tell you today to be on the alert, and do whatever the Lord tells you to do, even if it is strange." Yes, it was strange because how could we move forward given the reality of our financial circumstances? Then, on June 1 our bank account suddenly began recovering. How did that happen?!?

As our finances improved, we continued ministry in the high desert and, by faith, made arrangements to return to Hawaii for the annual apostolic conference in November.

I did not know at this point that I was to have a fiery encounter with the burning bush.

---

[1] Psalm 105:17-19 ESV

[2] Hartley, J. E. (1999). 1972 צָרַף. In R. L. Harris, G. L. Archer Jr., & B. K. Waltke (Eds.), *Theological Wordbook of the Old Testament* (electronic ed., p. 777). Moody Press.

[3] See Appendix

Chapter Six:
Expecting the Burning Bush

More promises from the Lord came and Rob Gross received this message from the Arcangel over the Kingdom Institute on July 25, 2023:

> Get ready for a major shift that will lift the Kingdom Institute out of the doldrums and into the fray. For the Great Shepherd, the Great I Am, is executing His plan to expand, build up and train His army for battle, and this is not prattle. This is the real deal, for the Great Shepherd shall extend His shepherds crook and draw the first wave of healers into battle, for the battle at this point is within the church. It is the paradigm that will get shifted and shifted to be trained up to destroy the works of the enemy because the Lord shall begin to shift the present-day mindset that has been lodged within the church for decades. The **fires of Elijah shall burn** in November for the hand of the Lord shall release a **burning fire** that will go deeper than the mind and will **burn up** the heart. The **Burning Man**[1] shall arise and light **fire** in the hearts of His people. **Fire** in His hands ignites, ignites, ignites. Ignition will pull down tradition. It's all about obedience and trust; trust is a must for it is about the Kingdom of God that is sure to come if My people will step out and trust the Lord.

Another promise came on September 13, 2023, delivered by the Kingdom Institute Archangel:[2]

> There are waves amassing offshore. These are waves of power, power for the hour from Him whom is a strong tower. Waves of power will crash upon the Kingdom Institute. Get ready for a massive release of Glory during November 9-12. In fact, you will begin to feel the power on November 8, for that will be a day of new beginning. The eleventh month will signify the eleventh hour. Read Deuteronomy 1:2-11, for on the eleventh day of the eleventh month the Lord instructed Moses at Kadesh Barnea. Head towards the promise land for, again, the 8th day represents new beginnings. Once again waves of power will hit the Kingdom Institute. **It is like the building will be shaken**. You will be shaken. Look for the throne room during the conference for the Power shall release waves of healing and waves of miracles. A new synergy will be released that will begin to bring the healers together, not just in Hawaii but globally for you are a royal priesthood in the hands of the Lord.

Another word on October 18, 2023, from the Kingdom Institute Archangel:

> On the 11th day of the 11th month of the 40th year, the Lord instructed Moses to go into the land. On November 11, you will experience a visitation from heaven. There is excitement in heaven over this, for there is a birthing of Kingdom activity that will ripple forth from the Kingdom Institute all the way back to Australia, England and beyond. The elements have been prepared, and fusion is about

to take place. This is Kingdom fusion. It is not an illusion; it is the real thing. A kingdom portal will open, and new levels of power will be released for the Lord's apostolic fleet has been commissioned and new territory will be conquered. This is a shift that will lift the fleet of the Lord to ride the wave of apostolic glory. This is only the beginning of the story so buckle up and let the wind of the Lord's spirit blow into your sail and go, go, go. Jesus is the great commander of this fleet and new territory will be conquered.

It shouldn't come as a surprise that anticipation for what the Lord had promised would happen was increasing. Then on November 6, 2023, another message:

Gird yourselves for you shall receive a visitation. You shall receive a supernatural visitation during the conference, and so I say to the two of you and to those who are at the conference, "Do not be afraid." For the Lord shall emerge out of the darkness and into the light. This will cause some of you to have a fright but rather, step into the light. It is all about the light. Line up to receive the light for the Lord shall dispense fresh balls of fire of His mighty desire that will unlock the gate into the greater glory weight. It will be tangible; you will feel it and it will reveal He who dwells in the darkness. Those who walk in the light will see the Lord who dwells in deep darkness. For you are the light of the world. You will be given the bright morning star to shine in dark places. Time is short; the clock is ticking. You have been given this light to penetrate darkness because time is short. There is a sense of urgency because time is accelerating in the spirit, for these are the days of Noah and time is ticking. **Fire, fire, fire of His desire**. How blessed are those who bring messages of good news.

But the Lord was still not finished! On November 6, yet another word came:

> The winds are blowing; the winds are swirling. It is a vortex of power off the shore that is building toward an hour of power. This will be a manifestation of the pool of Bethesda in their midst for the Lord shall commission those at the conference to heal the sick, do miracles and release the kingdom of God. This will be the greatest release of Power, Paul, that you have ever seen in any of the meetings you have been a part of for the last thirty hears. The switch will be flipped. Powers, rulers, the sun of righteousness, the Father of Power, Jesus as the Son of Man and the Holy Spirit shall all manifest, creating **nuclear fission** in the Spirit. You will never pass this way again. This will be a Holy moment in the Kingdom, for all of creation has been waiting for the manifestation of the sons of God. The countdown has begun for you and Rob are at Cape Carnival in the Spirit. This is ground zero; get ready for takeoff. **Warn the people to not be afraid of the Power**. Come up higher and experience the **fire of God's great desire.**

It was now November 8, 2023, and the Apostolic Conference was about to begin. I discerned that the Lord had instructed Moses to speak to us. This was to be the final word of preparation:

> You will never pass this way again. For decades, decades, decades you, Donna, Rob and many

others, it has felt like you have been going around and around and around. For decades, but now it is time to leave the wilderness and move steadily into the land of promise. There will be more strongholds that need to be defeated such as Jericho and other fortresses of the enemy; but nevertheless, it is time, God's time to begin the transition to a new position where you will start to experience a new level of power for the hour. I will manifest myself in the cloud in your midst for you have been faithful, Paul, to follow the cloud and the **pillar of fire**. The cloud will descend in your midst, it will manifest. This will be a life changing, life transforming, pivotal move of God. There will be a new level of authority that is imparted. (It feels like the statue of liberty, a torch.) A **fiery torch** that releases freedom to the captives will be given to the team that will release the nations. Get set for a season of new interest from new people, for the Lord is releasing a gathering anointing upon the Kingdom Institute. This is a now season. The rulers want to say yes and amen to everything that is being declared.

If you can, imagine Rob and I at this moment. After all of these words, Rob and I had vowed that we would not try to cause anything to happen. Only the Lord could do that and what He said, He would do. Still, we wondered what that would look like. Would He manifest like He said He would?

---

[1] The Burning Man is Jesus, as referenced in Daniel 10:6 and Revelation 1:12-16

[2] Prophetic words/messages are often delivered by angels who are God's messengers. Over the years we have also received messages from other spiritual beings, including archangels and often an archangel seems to be assigned to a particular ministry or area (i.e., an archangel over Aslan's Place or California, etc.)

Chapter Seven:
Encountering the Burning Bush

It was now Saturday morning, November 11, 2023. The Lord had richly blessed our times together but the words about the fire falling had not yet been realized. Lunch was served, and the afternoon session had begun. I shared a PowerPoint presentation about God's Grace, and we discerned a new gate called Grace. Then another gate was discerned - it was a gate of the burning bush.

There were no more words about the future, but a 'now word' from the Lord came before we began to walk through the gate.

> Rejoice, oscillate, rejoice, for I have broken the parts that bind your roots. I have shaken the soil that is dead, and I have called you upwards to beneath the shadow of my throne. Here you are secure, here is provision, and there is more, and I say to you, "Do not come down, do not come down, do not come down. Stay in this place, remain here, do not come down to the field of 'oh no'. Remain beneath the shadow of my throne and see what I will do, see what I will bring, see what I will show, see what I will destroy and call in my kingdom throne.

> You are the depths of His love, for the Father loves each of you more than you will ever realize or understand. This you must know first and foremost; you are loved unconditionally and there

is a battle cry in the land, not only in Hawaii but also in Australia and England and in every state that you have come from. I will no longer tolerate what has been going on in the world. I am coming with a **fire.** It is the roar of Aslan [Turkish word for lion], and a wave of healing power will sweep across your respective venues, respective lands from where you have come."

I am going to place the miraculous in and through you. Do you believe this? Do you believe this? There is power for the hour. A gate of power and a gate of grace for the race ahead. Convergence has taken place right here, right now. For this season, I will light up the land with **My fire**, the earth will move, and the sons and daughters of God shall arise and shall be revealed. This is a holy moment, for you shall never pass this way again. Moses took off his shoes, and **you are at the burning bush**. This is a holy moment for the I am sending you into your respective 'Egypts' to set the captives free. I am saying to the pharaohs of the land, "Set my people free!"

(Rob speaking) Offshore to your right and to my left, right offshore the waves are building, the waves are rolling in. Get ready for **nuclear fission** for the vision because people are going to face the reality that there is a valley of decision in which they must choose the Lord in this hour.

I am here, I see your hearts, I hear your cries, I have heard you. Have you heard me? Have you heard me? Have you heard me in the whisper, in the wind, when you were speaking to that friend or to family members. You are mine; I have called you to this place. For this time is the time for you to move, it is time for you to take what I have given, and I have given you much, I have equipped you. It is time to move; it is time to step out. I love you; I will never leave or forsake you, but this is a call to war, a call to action; and it will take everything of you, but I am with you, you are mine, you are my people and there are so many of you and you are all mine. There are many who are still not mine yet, I love them, I love all of you. I want more. You are the ones I have equipped, you can see, hear, feel, touch, taste; you discern, you know, so go out and touch those around you. Feel my love and share my love with them because they need you now. The enemy is moving, do you not see he is moving? He is already implementing his plans. It is time to implement mine. My plans are greater, for I am the strategist. I see what he does. I have put you in this time, this place, because you have a part of the strategy; you are part of My strategy so the enemy cannot know, he cannot hear what I say to you because he does not know me. When you move, he must react because there are so many of you who know Me and move. He cannot be victorious. Do you not see that I have given you part of the bigger picture, that you are all valuable? If not one of you does your part, the plan does not go as I strategized. There are always others, but you don't want to be one who is replaced. Be a part of this because I love you and have called you. Hear Me in the winds, in the silence, hear Me in the quiet, hear Me. I love you; I will never forsake you, but I will give you the strength and the courage to face the hardships; so be prepared, it will not be easy, it is not a simple plan. It will take everything in you, but I am with you; hear me, hear me.

(Rob speaking) The Lord of harvest is here and is equipping us for the harvest. The Spirit of the Fear of the Lord is here. This is why we had to receive the charge from Paul. Do you consent to do the work? Because once you consent, there is no take back; when you go through the gate, you have become the greater fleet so that the harvest can come. It is total death to yourself, plans, kingdom, everything you ever wanted to do. Take these tools that the Lord of harvest is giving us, that we must use; be accountable to give and take these anointings, gifts, callings He has equipped us with. This is His story now, there is no more control for us; we must continue to die so we can live because that's the only way forward. We must move with the Spirit that gives life, the flesh is no help at all.

We invited the attendees to walk through the gate and the 'fire of Elijah' fell on us. There was wreckage everywhere as wave after wave of Power fell upon us. Rob and I walked through the gate, and I found myself plastered to the floor of the building. Rob was also pinned to the ground. In a moment, my life was totally changed.

The next day, Sunday, a local resident of Oahu, shared that just after the Saturday encounter, she called her cousin who was incarcerated in Halawa Correctional Facility, which is literally next door to the church facility. The prisoner asked her if she had felt the earthquake on Saturday. Mystified, she reported she had not. Her cousin replied, "All of the prisoners here felt the earth shake." The time he reported was exactly when the burning bush gate manifested. He asked her if she knew what this meant, and she shared what had happened and spoke of the Lord. That day he gave his life to the Lord. Jesus had just set a prisoner free.

The burning bush had been revealed again - as promised. My own personal burning intensified and continued. I had waited long enough to see the fire of Elijah come.

Fire: The Furious Burning Love of Our Bridegroom

CHAPTER EIGHT:
BURNING, BURNING, BURNING...

As described previously, the physical sensation of burning had begun for me on June 5, 2022, and had gradually intensified to a point that was almost unbearable. It was like a blow torch scorching my back and I would often scream into my pillow from the pain. It was now January 19, 2024, and I had been burning for nineteen months and two weeks with no clear understanding of what was occurring in my life.

I traveled to Winston-Salem, North Carolina to conduct a weekend seminar at Awake Church with Dawn Bray, the Pastoral Care Pastor. After she picked me up at the airport, we went to Crackle Barrel for dinner, and I shared my frustration and confusion over not understanding the continued nights of burning. Dawn then said, "I just started burning. Oh my, I remember a dream I had about encountering John the Baptist." She shared the dream, which happened on June 18, 2022, just after I had first begun burning:

> I was sitting beside a lady wearing green in a community or church setting. Then I went outside to the parking lot and met John the Baptist. He was wearing linen (like the clothes from Bible times/the Chosen). He had deep brown eyes and smiled. John locked eyes with me in a serious way said, "By now I would have thought you'd be all oil and fire." It was an intense word but felt like an invitation. As

we stood there, a lady approached us who was demonized. John and I both pointed and spoke something together and she was set free. Then John and I began to walk together, and I laid my head against his shoulder and began to cry and pray "Father, help." The lady we spoke over was now following us, as well as others. We walked past a lady lying on the ground in a dress with a small flower pattern. I saw movement in the Spirit over her and pointed to it and asked John, "What is that?" He said, "She has the glory cloud around her." I was discerning in my body as we engaged together in different situations. I heard someone call my name, Dawn, and as I turned to see who called, I woke up.

Awake, it felt like the Lord had called my name and it awakened me.

This experience was so real, as if I'd been with an old friend (John).

In the Spirit, I could clearly see a vision of what looked like the tarmac at an airport with oil and flames coming up from it, and I could feel/discern the burning in my body. This was the beginning of the burning season for me, and since this night the oil and flames and burning have continued.

A few days later I had an experience/encounter while I was awake, spending time with the Lord. John the Baptist and Jesus with a dove sitting on his shoulder walked into the room. I knelt and they put their hands on my head, praying over me. Then they touched each of my shoulders with a sword and as I was helped to stand they put new sandals on my feet (that were not to come off). I knew there was a baptism of fire, the Fear of the Lord and burning love (like a seal). The dove flew from Jesus' shoulder to my shoulder, and I walked forward with them.

The following morning, Dawn called me and said she had been up most of the night listening to the Lord speak of the burning. She shared this word from the Lord.

> Feeling the burning and power
>
> My presence is upon you burning one
>
> My power is coming to rest on you
>
> The weight of my glory
>
> Who can withstand the weight of my glory?
>
> Those who are oil and fire My burning ones
>
> (Thought of Malachi 3:2: *But who can endure the day of his coming, and who can stand when he appears? For he is like a refiner's fire and like fullers' soap.*)
>
> The fire, the fire
>
> The glory and the fire
>
> The power
>
> The power
>
> In the glory and the fire

I was stunned! Of course, Malachi 3 and 4 speak of the fire of God and the intensity that comes from the burning of the furnace.

That night we began a conference at Awake Church and the Lord spoke again to us about the burning and the fire.

There's a fire coming through the eyes
There's a purification that's happening
There's a purification taking place through the eyes, through the vision
There's a purity that is coming
There is a cleansing that is taking place
You just read it in Malachi
Refiners soap to purify
(My head is on fire, coming off, feet burning)
Also, there's fire being released off your tongue
As you speak, you will speak with tongues of fire
It's the fire of the Holy Spirit being released
As you speak this fire will go into others and set them free because the fire will continue
Burning, rolling off, brings deliverance and healing
Temperature turned up
Even the ears, the hearing will be cleansed
The fire is consuming (going down the body)
Prepare ye the way of the Lord
Behold I am coming
I am coming now as a refiner's fire
I am coming through every dimension
Through every window
Through every door
Through every gate
Through every portal
Through every single dimension

> My fire will burn up all that has kept you from My power
>
> For I must release My power upon the land
>
> I must release My power on My people
>
> I must release My power
>
> I must, I must, I must, I must, I must
>
> He's burning up the dross

Dawn continued: All the impurities are being burned up so you will come as fine gold, and what you release out of fine gold is His presence to others. You carry His presence and He's removing the dross, the distractions, the doubts and fears that have built up. He's removing that so you can come forth shining with His glory He's the fire. Don't be afraid; let this wash over you, refine and cleanse you.

He is inviting us to this place, and He is weeping because of the things that have stopped us up. His power hasn't been able to flow freely, and He is inviting us to let it go, shake it off. It's ok. You are safe. Do not be afraid.

I knew I needed to revisit my understanding of Malachi 3 and 4. It seemed that I was living what the prophet had prophesied over two thousand years ago.

Chapter Nine:
The Furnace

My journey with the furnace started during the initial stages of the development of Aslan's Place's foundation. After the revelation of the furnace, the Lord instructed us to hold a tent meeting at the Victorian house in Hesperia. It was a very hot desert day, and about 70 people gathered in the tent on a weekday. That evening the furnace manifested and I invited people to come to the front to walk into the furnace. A man who later became a good friend walked through the furnace and was healed of brain cancer.

Sometime later, I was in Germany ministering in a small church in Munich and told the pastor, "I believe the Lord has shown us a key to healing with the furnace." He was not convinced, and I forgot the conversation. Now I realize that perhaps I was right but had no idea that it would take another 20 years to understand the veracity of my statement.

In 2007, we published the book, *Heaven Trek: Daring to Go Where God Wants You to Go*. In this book I provided a history of my revelation of the furnace, which I will also share here.

Some time ago in *Christianity Today*, there was a little vignette that was part of a collection of sayings on one page. As I read one paragraph, I was shocked. This excerpt had been taken from a book written by Annie Dillard, who wrote, "Why is it that we come to church like children playing with a chemistry set? Should we not come to church with crash helmets and seat belts because perhaps one day the God of the universe might come and visit His church?"

I have never forgotten her words, for they express a very valid concern regarding the way many of us are used to doing church. Again, I can say that things have changed for me because God has seriously altered my perception of how we are to come to Him and experience Him in church.

Donna and I were attending a conference in Mar de Plata, Argentina. Many smaller churches had come together as one large congregation. It was an unusual situation because the pastors in the city worked together to build the Kingdom of God, not just their own local church. We had tried to stay in the back, but Ed Silvoso insisted that we come and sit in the front row of an almost-full auditorium on the platform that seated about 1500 people. On the platform, Cindy Jacobs was taking the offering. There I was, just minding my own business, when she came and sat down between her husband, Mike, and me. I looked at her and said, "Cindy, there is a furnace on your head." She looked at me with a funny expression as if I had just had one too many drinks and turned away as if I had not said anything, probably thinking, "Poor Paul, he's really lost it."

Meanwhile, I was trying to pay attention to the speaker, but all the while thinking, "What is this? It is something new, but I don't know what it is." On my head I could feel a sensation that was like a blast furnace with the hot air rising up. It was the furnace.

After the service, speaking to a friend who is incredibly discerning, I said, "I think I feel a furnace. Do you know what that is?" He replied, "I saw it! I saw it! It was sitting right in the front of the auditorium. It was this very big furnace." I thought, "Well, that's interesting, but now what?" For me, discernment does not come with an instruction manual. I would have to wait for further understanding.

Sometime later, ministering in a little church in Northern California at a weekend seminar, the crowd swelled to forty on Friday night, and I was sitting there feeling the furnace again. I stood up and said the words that are terrifying to a pastor, "I don't know what I'm going to do. I think God wants us to learn something." Not knowing what else to do, I said, "I think we're all supposed to stand." So, all forty of us stood. Listening to the Lord while trying to figure out what was going on, I turned to look at the pastor, who was standing to my right, and suddenly he fell to the ground and started shaking. I thought, "Well this is interesting!" Soon people started falling everywhere. Then, I also fell to the ground. Just visualize this. I fell in such a position that my face was right up close to the face of the pastor. As I lay there shaking, I told him, "This is a fine mess. The two guys who oversee this meeting are on the ground and we cannot get up." As I looked around at everyone else on the floor, I discerned demonic beings leaving. "The Lord has come, and He is doing a sovereign deliverance on people," I said. The Lord had begun a new adventure in my life; – He'd started doing group deliverances.

The next part of my 'furnace journey' took place during a ministry trip to Switzerland. A guest speaker from Africa was scheduled to preach on the last Sunday morning that I was there but he was unable to come. A friend of mine was going to take his place, but as we were having breakfast, he turned to me and asked, "Do you have anything for this morning?" Initially I did not think so, but then the awesome power of God fell upon both of us, and I said, "Oh, I think I might have something." We went to church, but I still did not know what was happening. Suddenly, God started downloading a sermon. First, He reminded me of some things I had previously studied and then started giving me new material. Now, understand that I am the guy who used to spend up to twenty-five hours a week reading all the commentaries for a sermon. Now, the Holy Spirit was downloading information as fast as I could write. It all had to do with Malachi 3 and 4, and I believe we are now living in the days described there.

As I taught on Malachi 3 and 4, waves of the Holy Spirit began to fall on us. As I concluded, the glorious presence of the Lord fell and again, the Lord initiated a group deliverance. Many were set free from generational bondage.

Notice what is revealed in Malachi:

> *"Behold, I send my messenger, and he will prepare the way before me. And the Lord whom you seek will suddenly come to his temple; and the messenger of the covenant in whom you delight, behold, he is coming, says the* L<small>ORD</small> *of hosts. But who can endure the day of his coming, and who can stand when he appears? For he is like a refiner's fire and like fullers' soap. He will sit as a refiner and purifier of silver, and he will purify the sons of Levi and refine them like gold and silver, and they will bring offerings in righteousness to the* L<small>ORD</small>*... "For behold, the day is coming, burning like an oven, when all the arrogant and all evildoers will be stubble. The day that is coming shall set them ablaze, says the* L<small>ORD</small> *of hosts, so that it will leave them neither root nor branch. But for you who fear my name, the sun of righteousness shall rise with healing in its wings. You shall go out leaping like calves from the stall. And you shall tread down the wicked, for they will be ashes under the soles of*

your feet, on the day when I act, says the LORD *of hosts."*[1]

---

[1] Malichi 3:1-3, 4:1-3

Chapter Ten:
Introducing the Linen Man

The Lord has patiently taught me over the years to do what the Father is doing. The lesson has been difficult to learn but as I have matured, I have discovered that 'following the cloud' leads to many serendipity moments of discovery, which explode into a cascade of astounding. May 5, 2022, was such a moment.

A friend called me to report that she'd just experienced a vision she did not understand:

> On Thursday morning, May 5, 2022, I was walking from one room to another in my home. As I was walking toward the doorway, I walked 'through' something. I then 'saw' in my mind's vision two burning eyes, red like burning coals, that just burned through what I thought was my brain, head, or mind.
>
> Whatever I had experienced exited out the back of my head and down my neck with some sort of surge, but not like that of electricity. It was the feeling of literally walking through something that was tangible, yet invisible.
>
> The burning eyes remained in my mind's vision, and I felt a pain above my brow on the right side. The eyes, I believed, were that of a person or being. The presence lingered for a long time with tingling pressure on the back, left, top side of my head, and with the eyes constantly burning.

What came to mind was Daniel by the River Tigress when he had been fasting and a semblance of a man with eyes of fire appeared (Daniel 10:4-6). I wondered what had just happened and why.

When I pray for Paul, I often get vision and/or feeling. Therefore, I was not quite sure if this was for me to unravel or if I was seeing something related to Paul or Aslan's Place ministry. I contacted him and asked, "Is the man with burning eyes in Daniel, the same as Revelation?" because I remembered the eyes of flaming fire in Revelation 1:14 and Revelation 19:12 as belonging to Jesus but was not sure that the two were the same.

Thereafter began the process of discernment and study to figure out who the man that I originally called the 'Burning Man" and now labeled the 'Linen Man'.

I remembered clearly the Daniel 10 passage as I had taught it many times over the previous several years, convinced what I had taught was correct; that being that Daniel was describing an encounter with a powerful, terrifying created being who had been sent by the Lord God. It was now several days later as I was reviewing the passage that I was mortified to discover I had totally misinterpreted the experience of Daniel. The verse that convinced me I had not understood the identity of the heavenly visitor is Daniel 10:6:

> *His body was like beryl, his face like the appearance of lightning, his eyes like flaming torches, his arms and legs like the gleam of burnished bronze, and the sound of his words like the sound of a multitude.*

All the characteristics of this being would fit into an understanding that this was a creation of the Lord except one. Only the Lord God has **the sound like the voice of a multitude**. This man in dressed in linen is the Lord, not a created being. I had leaped into a new realm of understanding, which would rock my world.

On July 27, 2022, I was coaching a group in North Carolina via zoom when the Lord took us to throne room. I could feel the River of Life, the River of God, flowing. Suddenly the discernment of the river changed to a sensation of a very rapid raging river with the speed of a waterfall. I felt that there was a new surge of the river with great healing present and then felt a new discernment. I realized the Lord had just given to me a tactile awareness on my head, which was discernment of the 'Man in Linen'.

August 8, 2022, was a day of new understanding when a friend emailed me a word about the Linen Man:

> The Linen Man is not a man but is like a man who is omnipotent and bright and full of color, unafraid of fire and bold for GOD alone. For HE is GOD and a part of one TRINITY, part of the triune GOD. The Linen Man is full of truth, full of life and full of insights for one to face. Why is this important for this day? Because of supernatural things the Linen Man can do, so come and walk with Me and be a part of the Triune; co-create with US. To know who you are following you must trust! It is not a secret to whom I AM, for I AM WHO I AM!
>
> Be not afraid to walk the distance with Me for I will give you supernatural ways and supernatural thoughts that will change the ways of what is misleading, and discomfort to those who oppose.

> For the Linen Man is not afraid to disclose what is truth. Vibrate with Me, dance with Me, sing with Me and know you are never alone from Me. I am your Savior, your Healer and your Knower of all. I AM EL SHADDI, the GOD ALMIGHTY who comes to deliver and set the captive free. So, walk with Me in the fiery deep and be not afraid to walk with Me beneath the deep! The dawn of day is a fiery place to see my covenants take place. You are the apple of My eye so please know I will not mislead you or misguide you. I will lead you to uncover come what is hidden beneath the deep.

My burning had started only a few weeks before, and now I was on an odyssey to explore the 'Man in Linen' in God's word. This new discovery of how far off my understanding of Daniel 10 had been really humbled me. How many other scriptures have I misinterpreted? Let's look at the verses that reveal truth about the 'Man in Linen' in the order of historical revelation.

Our exploration begins in Ezekiel 8:1-2:

> *And it came to pass in the sixth year, in the sixth month, on the fifth day of the month, as I sat in my house with the elders of Judah sitting before me, that the hand of the Lord GOD fell upon me there. Then I looked, and there was a likeness, like the appearance of fire—from the appearance of His waist and downward, fire; and from His waist and upward, like the appearance of brightness, like the color of amber.*
>
> *In the sixth year, in the sixth month, on the fifth day of the month, as I sat in my house, with the elders of Judah sitting before me, the hand of the Lord GOD*

> *fell upon me there. Then I looked, and behold, a form that had the appearance of a man. Below what appeared to be his waist was fire, and above his waist was something like the appearance of brightness, like gleaming metal. (ESV)*

In this passage the phrase 'Man in Linen' is not used but the description is the same. Initially, Ezekiel says the one he saw was *a form that had the appearance of a man.*

> Ezekiel was very careful never to say that he saw God, *ĕlōhîm* (as did Isaiah in his prophecy, Isa 6:1, the object or content of Isaiah's vision is *ădōnāy*), but only that he saw the likeness of God."[1]

We are told that His form was like a man. The text does not say that He is a man, but that his form and likeness is comparable to a man. Below what seemed to be His waist there was a 'brightness', the same word used in Daniel 12:3 that means 'shall shine like the brightness of heaven'. What is the brightness like? 'Gleaming metal,' which in modern Hebrew is the word for electricity. In ancient Hebrew, it was translated as 'amber'. The word conveys a sense of brilliance and divine glory, especially given that the temperature of hot amber would be 393-716 degrees Fahrenheit.

We would be remiss if we didn't explain why the Linen Man appears now in Ezekiel. His appearance reveals to Ezekiel the terrible sins of his nation as the Linen Man comes to expose what only the Lord sees. He is a just God and He will not tolerate the hidden sins of mankind.

> *Then He said to me, "Son of man, lift your eyes now toward the north." So I lifted my eyes toward the north, and there, north of the altar gate, was this image of jealousy in the entrance. Furthermore He*

> said to me, "Son of man, do you see what they are doing, the great abominations that the house of Israel commits here, to make Me go far away from My sanctuary? Now turn again, you will see greater abominations." So He brought me to the door of the court; and when I looked, there was a hole in the wall. Then He said to me, "Son of man, dig into the wall"; and when I dug into the wall, there was a door. And He said to me, "Go in, and see the wicked abominations which they are doing there." So I went in and saw, and there—every sort of creeping thing, abominable beasts, and all the idols of the house of Israel, portrayed all around on the walls. And there stood before them seventy men of the elders of the house of Israel, and in their midst stood Jaazaniah the son of Shaphan. Each man had a censer in his hand, and a thick cloud of incense went up. Then He said to me, "Son of man, have you seen what the elders of the house of Israel do in the dark, every man in the room of his idols? For they say, 'The LORD does not see us, the LORD has forsaken the land.'" And He said to me, "Turn again, and you will see greater abominations that they are doing."[2]

We had now experienced our introduction to the Linen Man, but it was only beginning and there was much more yet to come.

---

[1] Hamilton, V. P. (1999). 437 ד. מ. ה. In R. L. Harris, G. L. Archer Jr., & B. K. Waltke (Eds.), *Theological Wordbook of the Old Testament* (electronic ed., p. 191). Moody Press.

[2] Ezekiel 8:5-13

Chapter Eleven:
EXPLORING THE LINEN MAN

The next stop on the journey of exploration regarding the Linen Man was Ezekiel 9:1-11:

> *Then He called out in my hearing with a loud voice, saying, "Let those who have charge over the city draw near, each with a deadly weapon in his hand." And suddenly six men came from the direction of the upper gate, which faces north, each with his battle-ax in his hand. One man among them was clothed with linen and had a writer's inkhorn at his side. They went in and stood beside the bronze altar. Now the glory of the God of Israel had gone up from the cherub, where it had been, to the threshold of the temple. And He called to the man clothed with linen, who had the writer's inkhorn at his side; ⁴ and the LORD said to him, "Go through the midst of the city, through the midst of Jerusalem, and put a mark on the foreheads of the men who sigh and cry over all the abominations that are done within it." To the others He said in my hearing, "Go after him through the city and kill; do not let your eye spare, nor have any pity. Utterly slay old and young men, maidens and little children and women; but do not come near anyone on whom is the mark; and begin at My sanctuary." So they began with the elders who were before the temple. Then He said to them, "Defile the temple, and fill the courts with the slain. Go out!" And they went out and killed in the city. So it was, that while they were killing them, I was left alone; and I fell on my face and cried out, and said, "Ah, Lord GOD! Will*

> *You destroy all the remnant of Israel in pouring out Your fury on Jerusalem?" Then He said to me, "The iniquity of the house of Israel and Judah is exceedingly great, and the land is full of bloodshed, and the city full of perversity; for they say, 'The LORD has forsaken the land, and the LORD does not see!' And as for Me also, My eye will neither spare, nor will I have pity, but I will recompense their deeds on their own head." Just then, the man clothed with linen, who had the inkhorn at his side, reported back and said, "I have done as You commanded me."*

We now had new understanding about the Linen Man - He is within and surrounded by the glory of the Lord. The Hebrew word for glory, *kābôd,* and its derivatives occur 376 times in the Hebrew Bible. Ezekiel reminds us here that his initial vision in Ezekiel 1 is pertinent to the Linen Man. This appearance is of One who is on the throne and rides on the Cherubim and has <u>a writer's inkhorn</u>.

> [This inkhorn} is usually a flat case about nine inches long, by an inch and a quarter broad, and half an inch thick, the hollow of which serves to contain the reed pens and penknife. At one end is the ink-vessel which is twice as heavy as the shaft. The latter is passed through the girdle and prevented from slipping through by the projecting ink-vessel. The whole is usually of polished metal, brass, copper or silver. The <u>man with the inkhorn</u> has to write in the Book of Life the names of those who shall be marked. The metaphor is from the custom of registering the names of the Israelites in public rolls.[1]

We now see the Linen Man as one who has the authority and position to judge mankind. The fear of the Lord fell on Elijah as he witnessed the just execution of judgment against sin. Also note that the Linen Man obeyed the direction of Elohim, which harkens to the relationship of Jesus to His Father in heaven while He was physically on the earth.

Ezekiel continued to unravel the mysteries of the Linen Man in Ezekiel 10:2-6:

> *And I looked, and there in the firmament that was above the head of the cherubim, there appeared something like a sapphire stone, having the appearance of the likeness of a throne. Then He spoke to the man clothed with linen, and said, "Go in among the wheels, under the cherub, fill your hands with coals of fire from among the cherubim, and scatter them over the city." And he went in as I watched. Now the cherubim were standing on the south side of the temple when the man went in, and the cloud filled the inner court. Then the glory of the LORD went up from the cherub, and paused over the threshold of the temple; and the house was filled with the cloud, and the court was full of the brightness of the LORD's glory. And the sound of the wings of the cherubim was heard even in the outer court, like the voice of Almighty God when He speaks. Then it happened, when He commanded the man clothed in linen, saying, "Take fire from among the wheels, from among the cherubim," that he went in and stood beside the wheels. And the cherub stretched out his hand from among the cherubim to the fire that was among the cherubim, and took some of it and put it into the hands of the man clothed with linen, who took it and went out.*

The Lord continued to unfold new layers of exposure about the preincarnate manifestation of our Lord: First, the Linen Man is high and lifted up and is associated with the Throne of God. Translators reveal the Hebrew words for the throne as 'a sapphire stone': "The people of biblical times probably did not understand the word to be the very hard modern sapphire, but lapis lazuli, the rich, azure gem so common to the ancient world."[2]

Next, a conversation transpired, and the Linen Man was told to go to the wheels under the cherubim and take burning[3] coals scatter them over the city. Who instructed the Lord to do this? I would suggest it was Elohim in conversation with the now-revealed Son of God, described the Son of Man in Daniel. Consider the fact that the temperature of burning coals is 1,000–3500 degrees Fahrenheit in the physical realm, yet it easily held in the hands of both the cherubim and the Man in Linen. The cherubim were now hovering over the 'house', which was the temple. The cloud manifested and the brightness (*nogah*), and the glory of the Lord was now present.

> The Hebrew word 'Nogah' primarily denotes a sense of brightness or radiance. It is often used in the context of light that is intense and shining, conveying a sense of splendor or glory. This term is used to describe both physical light and metaphorical light, such as the glory of God or the radiance of His presence."[4]

Our world has totally misunderstood the power and might of Elohim. He is not a bland God, but He is <u>the Power</u> who sits on the throne; He is the God who is <u>an all-consuming fire.</u> His Son, the Linen Man, cannot be totally described. The words listed in Ezekiel - glory, burning coals, fire, brightness, radiance, and electric - are inadequate attempts to explore the power and visual awe of the Living God.

And yet, there's even more!

---

[1] Barnes, A. (1879). <u>Notes on the Old Testament: Proverbs, Ecclesiastes, Song of Solomon, Jeremiah, Lamentations & Ezekiel</u> (F. C. Cook & J. M. Fuller, Eds.; p. 325). John Murray.

[2] Patterson, R. D. (1999). <u>1535 סָפִיר</u>. In R. L. Harris, G. L. Archer Jr., & B. K. Waltke (Eds.), *Theological Wordbook of the Old Testament* (electronic ed., p. 631). Moody Press.

[3] 'esh /aysh

[4] https://biblehub.com/hebrew/5052.htm

CHAPTER TWELVE:
DANIEL AND THE LINEN MAN

The Book of Daniel was probably written around 530 B.C., some years after Ezekiel. The unfolding revelation about the Linen Man crescendos to a sensational level in Daniel 10:4-9:

> *Now on the twenty-fourth day of the first month, as I was by the side of the great river, that is, the Tigris, I lifted my eyes and looked, and behold, a certain man clothed in linen, whose waist was girded with gold of Uphaz! His body was like beryl, his face like the appearance of lightning, his eyes like torches of fire, his arms and feet like burnished bronze in color, and the sound of his words like the voice of a multitude. And I, Daniel, alone saw the vision, for the men who were with me did not see the vision; but a great terror fell upon them, so that they fled to hide themselves. Therefore, I was left alone when I saw this great vision, and no strength remained in me; for my vigor was turned to frailty in me, and I retained no strength. Yet I heard the sound of his words; and while I heard the sound of his words, I was in a deep sleep on my face, with my face to the ground.*

This man was clothed in linen, which is the fabric from which the clothing of the high priest was made.[1] Studying this passage I asked the Lord, "Why linen?" I had the impression to look up what a bridegroom during the time of Jesus would wear to his wedding and wouldn't you know it? He would wear white linen, and here we see here

Jesus as our both our high priest and bridegroom. Around His waist is a gold belt, which may have been:

> ...in the form of chain-links, hinged panels, or gold thread embroidery... A linen belt embroidered with gold thread is most likely. [A gold belt] was part of the costume of the wealthy and royal classes in the ancient Near East. In this context the symbolism may suggest a king or judge."[2]

> The Linen Man's body was like beryl. Beryl seemed to be some kind of gold-colored precious stone, although its exact identification is unclear. It might be compared to our topaz, a flashing stone like that of gold.' Some yellow-colored stone must have been intended because the term describes the body of the heavenly being as glowing. His face is the appearance of lighting. Movement is indicated here. In other words, lightning flashes from His face. David explains in Psalm 18:14 the same concept – "Lord flashed forth lightings." We are told by Moses that when he encountered God on Mt. Sinai his face "flashed forth light." His eyes were flaming torches." "His arms" and "legs" gleamed like "burnished bronze," indicating that his body had a fiery appearance, like burning metal.[3]

I wondered at the heat/temperature of what Daniel saw. Lightning can reach 50,000 degrees Fahrenheit, bronze 1900 degrees Fahrenheit, and a flaming torch also burns at 1900 degrees Fahrenheit. Truly, He is the burning man.

There was not just a visual understanding. There was a great and awesome sound, **the sound of his words like the sound of a multitude**. The Hebrew word *hemyâ* is translated as 'sound' or 'music'. This root, used thirty-four times, means 'cry out', 'make a loud noise', or 'be turbulent'. It is a strong word, emphasizing unrest, commotion, strong feeling, or noise.[4]

I shared earlier that I had not really understood who was involved in Daniel 10, so I would like to relate what I now believe happens next in the text - a new being is now revealed in Daniel 10:10:

> *Suddenly, a hand touched me, which made me tremble on my knees and on the palms of my hands. And he said to me, "O Daniel, man greatly beloved, understand the words that I speak to you, and stand upright, for I have now been sent to you." While he was speaking this word to me, I stood trembling Then he said to me, "Do not fear, Daniel, for from the first day that you set your heart to understand, and to humble yourself before your God, your words were heard; and I have come because of your words. But the prince of the kingdom of Persia withstood me twenty-one days; and behold, Michael, one of the chief princes, came to help me, for I had been left alone there with the kings of Persia. Now I have come to make you understand what will happen to your people in the latter days, for the vision refers to many days yet to come." When he had spoken such words to me, I turned my face toward the ground and became speechless.*

This angelic being arrived on the twenty-fourth day after Daniel's initial prayer, having warred with evil for all that time. If Jesus as the manifested Linen Man had been involved there would have been no war - He would have been instantly victorious. But I was not yet finished being surprised by how much I had misunderstood what was transpiring in Daniel 10. It seems there is also a third one in this drama.

> *And suddenly, one having the likeness of the sons of men touched my lips; then I opened my mouth and spoke, saying to him who stood before me, "My lord, because of the vision my sorrows have overwhelmed me, and I have retained no strength. For how can this servant of my lord talk with you, my lord? As for me, no strength remains in me now, nor is any breath left in me."* [5]

This new one is said to have *the likeness of the sons of men.* Who is he? I don't know, but it does seem to be someone else, a third being.

---

[1] Exodus 28:42; Lev 6:10

[2] Miller, S. R. (1994). *Daniel* (Vol. 18, pp. 280–281). Broadman & Holman Publishers.

[3] Miller, S. R. (1994). *Daniel* (Vol. 18, pp. 281–282). Broadman & Holman Publishers.

[4] Weber, C. P. (1999). 505 הָמָה. In R. L. Harris, G. L. Archer Jr., & B. K. Waltke (Eds.), *Theological Wordbook of the Old Testament* (electronic ed., p. 219). Moody Press.

[5] Daniel 10:16-17

CHAPTER THIRTEEN:
DANIEL'S CONCLUSION

Daniel concluded his understanding about the Linen Man in the final words of his book:

> *But you, Daniel, shut up the words, and seal the book until the time of the end; many shall run to and fro, and knowledge shall increase." Then I, Daniel, looked; and there stood two others, one on this riverbank and the other on that riverbank. And one said to the man clothed in linen, who was above the waters of the river, "How long shall the fulfillment of these wonders be?" Then I heard the man clothed in linen, who was above the waters of the river, when he held up his right hand and his left hand to heaven, and swore by Him who lives forever, that it shall be for a time, times, and half a time; and when the power of the holy people has been completely shattered, all these things shall be finished. Although I heard, I did not understand. Then I said, "My lord, what shall be the end of these things?" And he said, "Go your way, Daniel, for the words are closed up and sealed till the time of the end. Many shall be purified, made white, and refined, but the wicked shall do wickedly; and none of the wicked shall understand, but the wise shall understand.*[1]

Daniel began by saying there is a time at the end when Michael, the chief prince, will stand up. In 2010, I was in Hong Kong at a conference with my friend, Rob Gross. We had concluded our day and were enjoying an evening meal at the hotel restaurant. Suddenly, I felt Michael the archangel stand up, and said to Rob, "Michael just stood up! I think that is in the Bible somewhere?" Indeed, it is in Daniel 12:1:

> *At that time Michael shall stand up,*
> *The great prince who stands watch over the sons of your people;*
> *Such as never was since there was a nation,*
> *Even to that time.*
> *And at that time your people shall be delivered,*
> *Every one who is found written in the book.*

The scripture goes on to indicate that judgment will follow; and then Daniel was instructed to close the book of his revelation, which goes on to indicate that the future will see an increase of knowledge. We are there now.

Daniel's final vision as recorded in his book, was of the Linen Man, now standing above the waters of the river. I was curious about that phrase as it seemed odd that Daniel would refer to the 'waters' and not just 'water' and concluded that these are the 'waters' in the dimensions or heavenly places. It is very interesting that 'water' throughout the Old Testament is always in the plural. Through the Lord's revelation we have noted that when a spiritual gate[2] is seen, water is often seen flowing out of that gate.

There were two others present during this vision - one on each side of the riverbank - who I believe these two are the Angels of the Lord who are His personal attendants. A discussion about the future ensued and we are given clues regarding the precursor to the end times as the tribulation is described. Daniel wondered, *"... what shall be the end of these things?"*[3] First, Daniel was instructed to seal up all the words he had written, and then the events prior to the end times were revealed:

> *Many shall be purified, made white, and refined, but the wicked shall do wickedly; and none of the wicked shall understand, but the wise shall understand.*[4]

When I first read this verse after so many months of burning, I finally understood what was happening to us. We are being refined, *bārar*, which means "purge, purify, choose, cleanse or make bright, test or prove".[5] ***Many shall be purified, made white, and refined...*** The Hebrew word for refined is *ṣārap*, meaning 'smelt, refine, test'. The context indicates what happens in the refining of gold and silver. The temperature in the refining of gold is 1832 to 2192 degrees Fahrenheit and the refining of silver is 1763 degrees Fahrenheit.

The Passion Translation captures the focus of this verse:

> *God will purify many people and make them clean and spotless, while the wicked will continue doing what is wicked. This revelation will remain a riddle to the wicked, but those who are wise will have profound understanding.*[6]

Many years ago, the Lord gave me a phrase to clarify what happens through discernment, "Revelation is only information until it is experienced and then it becomes a reality in my life." Often, we may read a verse but not fully grasp the depth of what it implies. Now, though discernment, I had learned that the process of refining, purifying, and being made white is not just an abstract concept. Rather, it is a reality of literal burning that is so intense one wonders if he/she can survive the process of purification, which ultimately leads to one becoming white. In the book of Revelation, we are told:

He who overcomes shall be clothed in white garments, and I will not blot out his name from the Book of Life; but I will confess his name before My Father and before His angels.[7]

Not only is Jesus clothed in white linen, but He imputes His righteousness to us, and we are also then dressed in white linen.

---

[1] Daniel 12:4-13

[2] We believe gates are entrances into the dimensions, or heavenly places.

[3] Daniel 12:8

[4] Daniel 12:10

[5] Kalland, E. S. (1999). 288 בָּרַר. In R. L. Harris, G. L. Archer Jr., & B. K. Waltke (Eds.), *Theological Wordbook of the Old Testament* (electronic ed., p. 134). Moody Press.

[6] Daniel 12:10 (TPT)

[7] Revelation 3:5; see also Revelation 3:18, 7:14, 7:9-17

Chapter Fourteen:
THE LITERAL WORD OF GOD

In seminary and graduate school, I was taught that the Bible is filled with figurative language, word pictures and figures of speech. In preaching, it is our responsibility to explore the nuances of the Hebrew, Aramaic, and Greek languages so that we can properly exegete each passage. Of course, this is often true but in my journey of discernment, I have discovered that the Bible is far more literal in the languages than we had first thought.

We have now come to the New Testament where Jesus has been resurrected from the dead and is appearing to many of His followers. Peter and others had been to the empty tomb where they found the folded while linen. Two of these unnamed followers were walking to Emmaus, a small village some seven miles north of Jerusalem, were discussing what had just happened in Jerusalem when Jesus came alongside and joined their conversation. He seemed curious as to what they understood had happened and when He'd heard enough, began to teach them:

> *Then He said to them, "O foolish ones, and slow of heart to believe in all that the prophets have spoken! Ought not the Christ to have suffered these things and to enter into His glory?" And beginning at Moses and all the Prophets, He expounded to them in all the Scriptures the things concerning Himself.*[1]

Arriving at their destination, Jesus stayed with them sat down to share a meal, first blessing the bread and then vanishing from their sight as their eyes were opened. Here, their observation resonated with me:

> *And they said to one another, "Did not our heart burn within us while He talked with us on the road, and while He opened the Scriptures to us?"*[2]

In my former Baptist days, I would have explained this away as a metaphor, a word picture describing what the two felt. No more! The Greek word for 'burn' *kaio*, which means "to set fire to, to light; to be lighted, to burn."[3] My sermon today regarding this passage would be much different. Doesn't it make sense that their hearts actually burned as if their bodies were actually set on fire? One cannot come into contact with the Living, Resurrected Christ and not walk away unaffected. The physical linen cloths remained in the grave but the holy linen clothes of the Man on Fire remain forever on Him.

The final leg of our journey in exploring the Man in Linen ends in Revelation 1:13-17:

> *...and in the midst of the seven lampstands One like the Son of Man, clothed with a garment down to the feet and girded about the chest with a golden band. His head and hair were white like wool, as white as snow, and His eyes like a flame of fire; His feet were like fine brass, as if refined in a furnace, and His voice as the sound of many waters; He had in His right hand seven stars, out of His mouth went a sharp two-edged sword, and His countenance was like the sun shining in its strength. And when I saw Him, I fell at His feet as dead. But He laid His right hand on me, saying to me, "Do not be afraid; I am the First and the Last.*

The apostle John has now disclosed new information about the Man in Linen. Note that linen is not used in the description of his garment; however, we are informed that the garment goes down to His feet. The gold band is on His chest, a sash, is like a belt. His head and hair are like wool. In Daniel, the Ancient of Days is also described as having a white garment with hair like wool, and as the Son of Man is presented before the Ancient of Days. We see here the mystery of the Trinity.

Jesus' eyes are like a flame of fire. 'Flame' in Greek is *phlox*, which means, 'to burn, shine as fire, a bright burning fire, or flame.' New information is again added here: Daniel described the Linen Man's legs as bronze while in Revelation, the Son of Man is said to have brass feet. Historically, brass and bronze are very similar but today the alloy is slightly different. Brass has a gold-like appearance that has mechanical, electrical, and chemical properties and its' melting point is 1,650 to 1720 degrees Fahrenheit. [4] It's not hard to understand that fire and burning are prevalent in the Burning Man.

His countenance, his face, is like the sun shining at full strength, which equates to about 10,000 degrees Fahrenheit. I have a sense that John found it difficult to describe the intensity of the burning of the Linen Man so perhaps he defaulted to simply saying that it was like the sun shining at full strength. The Holy Spirit chooses this word carefully. It is the sun at full power, *dunamis*. It is power in action; it is the power of miracles; it is power in 'full force'.[5]

He is not an impotent God, as He is often conceptualized by our modern world, but He is the 'Fiery One', Who will come with a sword in hand to render judgment on the earth, to right what is wrong, and to give to the ones whom he has 'burned up' the kingdoms of this world. Justice is coming for those who have chosen to follow Him - His burning will enter us and become our burning desire to follow our Bridegroom, after which He and His followers will reign forever and ever and ever:

> *I was watching in the night visions, And behold, One like the Son of Man, Coming with the clouds of heaven! He came to the Ancient of Days, and they brought Him near before Him. Then to Him was given dominion and glory and a kingdom, that all peoples, nations, and languages should serve Him. His dominion is an everlasting dominion, which shall not pass away, And His kingdom the one which shall not be destroyed.* [6]

The book of Daniel ends with end-times prophecy. Approximately a century later Malachi would write what we know as the final book of the Old Testament, a book in which fire and the Day of the Lord go hand-in-hand.

---

[1] Luke 24:25–27

[2] Luke 24:32

[3] Vine, W. E., Unger, M. F., & White, W., Jr. (1996). In *Vine's Complete Expository Dictionary of Old and New Testament Words* (Vol. 2, p. 84). T. Nelson.

[4] https://en.wikipedia.org/wiki/Brass

[5] 5 Vine, W. E., Unger, M. F., & White, W., Jr. (1996). In *Vine's Complete Expository Dictionary of Old and New Testament Words* (Vol. 2, p. 2). T. Nelson.

[6] Daniel 7:13–14

CHAPTER FIFTEEN:
FIRE & THE DAY OF THE LORD

> *Behold, I send My messenger, and He will prepare the way before Me. And the Lord, whom you seek, will suddenly come to His temple, even the messenger of the covenant, in whom you delight. "Behold, He is coming," says the Lord of Hosts. "But who can endure the day of His coming? And who can stand when He appears?" Malachi 3:1-2a*

It is generally believed that this is a "day of the Lord" passage.

> The DAY OF THE LORD expression used by OT prophets (as early as the eighth-century BC prophet Amos) to signify a time in which God actively intervenes in history, primarily for judgment. Thus "the day of the Lord" is also called "the day of the LORD's anger" (Zep 2:2). The term refers to climactic future judgment of the world (Jl 3:14-21; Mal 4:5). The final Day of the Lord is characterized in the Bible as a day of gloom, darkness, and judgment. Associated with God's judgment is language depicting changes in nature, especially a darkening of the sun, moon, and stars. Following the judgment, the future Day of the Lord will be a time of prosperity, restoration, and blessing for Israel (Joel 3:18-21).[1]

As we progress in our study of 'fire', you will notice a pattern in the scriptures that we emphasize. Many of them are end times passages. There seems to be a relationship between the release of the 'fire' and the end times.

Malachi 3 and 4 are typical of end times prophetic passages. The prophetic word can have an immediate application, a more recent future fulfilment and an end time final application. Malachi speaks of Jesus coming to the first century temple after preparation by John the Baptist. However, there is also a future coming that will bring 'fire'. This coming is so dramatic that we are warned that one may not be able to 'endure' that coming. Jeremiah uses the word in a figurative sense when he expresses the impossibility of containing within himself the Lord's fury, which is like a burning fire (Jer 6:11; 20:9).[2]

One can read the word 'endure' without experiencing the pain of the experience. I was such a person, for 'endure' was simply a word to me. But when the pain and intensity of the 'fire' came upon me night after night, week after week and year after year, in my anguish I was terrified that I would not survive the onslaught of the burning.

John the Baptist also told of a day that was coming, which would be the coming Messiah.

> *I indeed baptize you with water unto repentance, but He who is coming after me is mightier than I, whose sandals I am not worthy to carry. He will baptize you with the Holy Spirit and fire. His winnowing fan is in His hand, and He will thoroughly clean out His threshing floor, and gather His wheat into the barn; but He will burn up the chaff with unquenchable fire.* [3]

Jesus did release the baptism of the Holy Spirit, but what about the baptism of fire? Traditionally we have believed the baptism of fire was the same as the baptism of the Holy Spirit, but I now am pondering if this is accurate. Reading the New Testament and reviewing church history, I can find no evidence of the kind of burning that is now happening on the earth. Perhaps the recent Baptism of Fire is another evidence of the closeness to the Day of the Lord:

> It has been suggested that Jesus' "baptism of fire" alludes to "an eschatological stream of fire by which the wicked are consumed and the righteous refined. His support scripture is Zechariah 13:9 – *"I will bring the one-third through the fire, will refine them as silver is refined, and test them as gold is tested. they will call on My name, and I will answer them. I will say, 'This is My people'; and each one will say, 'The LORD is my God.' "*[4]
>
> This baptism of fire is the holiness of God, which consumes all that is inconsistent with His nature and divine judgment, testing the deeds of believers.[5]
>
> John the Baptist then enlists another image of what is on the agenda of Jesus. His winnowing fan is in His hand, and He will thoroughly clean out His threshing floor, and gather His wheat into the barn; but He will burn up the chaff with unquenchable fire.[6]
>
> The winnowing fork is the image of a farmer separating valuable wheat from worthless chaff by throwing the grain into the air and allowing the two constituent elements to separate in the wind. The wheat, like believers, is preserved and safeguarded; the chaff, like unbelievers, is destroyed in an unquenchable fire.[7]

The conclusion of this baptism of fire is during the final events of the Day of the Lord.

Going back to Malachi, he uses a comparison to explain what the fire is like - a refiner's fire. So, what is a refiner's fire like? In Malachi 3:3, the refiner's fire is like a fire that purifies silver and gold. That is a startling image because a refiner's fire for silver burns at 1600 to 1800 degrees Fahrenheit, and gold at 1948 degrees Fahrenheit. It is also like a fuller's soap:

> The reference is a form of lye, or potash, an extremely strong soap. This is the kind of material used to dissolve impurities and bleach clothes. Just as the refiner's fire removes what is impure, destroying what is undesirable so too does this 'fuller's soap' wash away stains and spots.[8]

Something happens during the process of refining and washing: There is a removal of impurities; there is a deliverance.

> According to G. A. Klingbeil, "God's refining of his people always involves a concrete goal or purpose, i.e., cleansing and purification. Something precious will result from the process."[9]

The focus of the purpose of the fire is on the tribe of Levi but there is a wider application:

> *Then the offering of Judah and Jerusalem will be pleasant to the* LORD, *as in the days of old, as in former years.*[10]

To the Lord, we are a holy priesthood, and He desires a pure priesthood, a priesthood refined in the fire.

Note that there are two groups involved in this purification, The recipients of the refining as well as those who are judged by the fire. This is the Lord's response to the impertinent question of Malachi 2:17, *"Where is the God of justice?"* Judgment is promised against six different groups of people:

> *And I will come near you for judgment;*
> *I will be a swift witness*
> *Against sorcerers,*
> *Against adulterers,*
> *Against perjurers,*
> *Against those who exploit wage earners and widows and orphans,*
> *And against those who turn away an alien—*
> *Because they do not fear Me,"*
> *Says the L*ORD *of hosts.*[11]

During my experience in the fire, I could feel an intense deliverance coming off my generational line. In the nighttime encounters, the Lord was removing the iniquity of my generational in my family line; the iniquity of all those mentioned above in the scripture.

Continuing in Malachi 3, it's clear that many were frustrated that the Lord was not doing anything to help them. Perhaps the encounter of the Lord coming as fire had not yet happened. There was a still a time of waiting and of expecting, but it had been so long in coming that frustration developed and truth regarding the goodness of the Lord was questioned:

> *"Your words have been hard against me, says the* L*ORD. But you say, 'How have we spoken against*

> *you?' You have said, 'It is vain to serve God. What is the profit of our keeping his charge or of walking as in mourning before the LORD of hosts?'[12]*

Now, be honest. Has that thought ever crossed our minds? Have you wondered at times if it really is worth serving God? We are now living in the day in which we are seeing an increased interest in the gift of healing; and yet, we pray and still have people dying. Yes, there are some wonderful sparks in places where fire is breaking out, but often we see nothing happen in answer to our prayers. We pray about our marriages; we pray about our families; we pray about our work situations; we pray about our ministries and our churches; we pray about so many things, and we ask, "What good has it been for us to pray about all these issues?" Then we wonder, "So what? I have a great time in church, but then I go home, and am miserable." Perhaps we begin thinking, "At least the sinners are not as miserable as we are; they're out having fun. Meanwhile, it seems like we must be, or act, spiritual in the Church, even while remaining miserable. Yes, they surely are having more fun than we are, and they don't feel guilty."

> *So now we call the proud blessed,*
> *For those who do wickedness are raised up;*
> *They even tempt God and go free.[13]*

Our society promotes celebrities, and it usually does not matter what they believe or do. The media does raise them up, proclaiming that it does not matter what they do or say. So yes, the proud are blessed today; and yet there is good news coming!

There are still those who love the Lord. Perhaps these are the ones who will now see the fire.

> *Then those who feared the* LORD *spoke with one another. The* LORD *paid attention and heard them, and a book of remembrance was written before him of those who feared the* LORD *and esteemed his name.*[14]

In essence, He was saying, "These are the people who have not given up on Me, those who meditate on My Name. They didn't give up." These are people of faith who, like Abraham, believed even though they never saw all the fulfillment of God's promises. These are the amazing people that trust even though they never had a reason to trust. These are people of faith who may be compared to the members of the Faith Hall of Fame in Hebrews 11.

> *"They shall be Mine," says the Lord of Hosts, "on the day that I make them My jewels [or translation My treasures in another translation], and I will spare them as a man spares his own son who serves him."* [15]

What is He saying? These people are so special to Me that they are like jewels. He looks down and sees the names of these people in the book of remembrance and says, "I remember now." He is always remembering our names, and He knows us intimately. King David said it well:

> *You saw who you created me to be before I became me! Before I'd ever seen the light of day, the number of days you planned for me were already recorded in your book. Every single moment you are thinking of me! How precious and wonderful to consider that you cherish me constantly in your every thought! O God, your desires toward me are more than the grains of sand on every shore! When I awake each morning, you're still with me.*[16]

The Lord now makes a remarkable statement! The result of patiently waiting on the Lord is discernment. Notice what happens on the day that the fire comes:

> ***Then you shall again discern between the righteous and the wicked, between the one who serves God and the one who does not serve Him.***[17]

You will begin to discern between good and evil, between the one who serves God and the one who does not serve Him. In other words, in the last days, the days of fire, the gift of discernment will be poured out upon God's people throughout the earth.

---

[1] Elwell, W. A., & Comfort, P. W. (2001). In *Tyndale Bible dictionary* (p. 362). Tyndale House Publishers.

[2] Oswalt, J. N. (1999). 962 כּוּל. In R. L. Harris, G. L. Archer Jr., & B. K. Waltke (Eds.), *Theological Wordbook of the Old Testament* (electronic ed., p. 432). Moody Press.

[3] Matthew 3:11-12

[4] Blomberg, C. (1992). *Matthew* (Vol. 22, p. 80). Broadman & Holman Publishers.

[5] Vine, W. E., Unger, M. F., & White, W., Jr. (1996). In *Vine's Complete Expository Dictionary of Old and New Testament Words* (Vol. 2, p. 239). T. Nelson.

[6] Matthew 3:12

[7] Blomberg, C. (1992). *Matthew* (Vol. 22, p. 80). Broadman & Holman Publishers.

[8] https://www.bibleref.com/Malachi/3/Malachi-3 2.html#:~:text=The%20reference%20is%20to%20a,wash%20away%20stains%20and%20spots.

[9] Taylor, R. A., & Clendenen, E. R. (2004). *Haggai, Malachi* (Vol. 21A, p. 389). Broadman & Holman Publishers.

Fire: The Furious Burning Love of Our Bridegroom

[10] Malachi 3:4
[11] Malachi 3:5
[12] Malachi 3:13-14 (ESV)
[13] Malachi 3:15
[14] Malachi 3:16 (ESV)
[15] Malachi 3:17
[16] Psalm 139:16-18 (TPT)
[17] Malachi 3:18

Chapter Sixteen:
FIRE - BLESSING OR JUDGMENT

Revisiting the truth of Malachi 3:2, there is an intense scorching that is coming, which will mark the Day of the Lord. This scaring fire will be so overpowering that it will be difficult to endure and will be like what firefighters call a flashover, a near-simultaneous ignition of all combustible materials in an area due to extreme heat usually around 1,100°F or 600°C. Literally everything not of the Lord will be eradicated, leaving only ashes as a reminder of what was once there.

Now, before looking more carefully at Malachi 4, it is valuable to remind ourselves that chapter divisions were not part of the original manuscripts. While is it is helpful to have chapter and verses, we are in error if we do not connect what has been written in one chapter in the context of the previous chapter.

Malachi was answering the complaint of the people as to why the Lord had not acted justly regarding the sin of the people. He reminds us that there are other individuals who are unlike those who complain that it is useless to follow the Lord (3:13-16). These committed followers of Yahweh do not give up on the Lord but are determined to follow Him (3:16). The result of this determination to preserve in the ways of their God will lead to a new outpouring of discernment, coupled with the ability to know good from evil. All of this is preparation for the yet-to-come Day of the Lord, which begins with burning

> The "day of the Lord: begins with burning. The Hebrew word "burn," *b 'r* means "to burn, blaze up, consume, scorch" (KBL 1:145–46). Oven, *tannûr* "is a fixed or portable earthenware stove, used especially for baking bread." This same word is use in Hosea 7:4 – "Hosea 7:4 "They *are* all adulterers. Like an oven heated by a baker, he ceases stirring *the fire* after kneading the dough, until it is leavened.[1]

David paints for us a vivid picture of this oven and the burning.

> *Your hand will find all Your enemies; Your right hand will find those who hate You. You shall make them as a fiery oven in the time of Your anger; The* LORD *shall swallow them up in His wrath, and the fire shall devour them. Their offspring You shall destroy from the earth, and their descendants from among the sons of men. For they intended evil against You; They devised a plot which they are not able to perform. Therefore You will make them turn their back; You will make ready Your arrows on Your string toward their faces. Be exalted, O* LORD, *in Your own strength! We will sing and praise Your power.* [2]

Note that the Lord only conveys to us a limited description of what this burning is like, which is because apparently human languages cannot describe the seriousness and depth of this burning and this fire. All that we can understand is that it is like an oven.

This judgment is coming suddenly on those who are arrogant; so proud that they are convinced no one sees their evil deeds and think they will escape without consequences.

However, there is a sudden event that will change the course of their wrenched lives:

> *"Your words have been harsh against Me," Says the LORD, Yet you say, 'What have we spoken against You?' You have said, 'It is useless to serve God; What profit is it that we have kept His ordinance, And that we have walked as mourners Before the LORD of hosts? So now we call the proud blessed, For those who do wickedness are raised up; They even tempt God and go free.' "*[3]

Isaiah 13:11 is another reminder of what is coming for those who do not consider the holiness of Elohim:

> *I will punish the world for its evil,*
> *And the wicked for their iniquity;*
> *I will halt the arrogance of the proud,*
> *and will lay low the haughtiness of the terrible.*

There is a frightening outcome to all this burning! The wicked will become 'stubble', which is the Hebrew word *qaš*. It is descriptive of grain chaff, stumps of grain stalks, straw stalks, or the like. The end result will be that there will be neither roots nor branches left. But what are the roots and branches?

Malachi now reminds us that the emphasis is not on the ones who are burned up but rather the spotlight is on the ones who fear His name:

> *But to you who fear My name*
> *The Sun of Righteousness shall arise*
> *With healing in His wings;*
> *And you shall go out*
> *And grow fat like stall-fed calves.*

Something wonderful is going to occur in this end-of-time period: The Sun of Righteousness will be revealed.

I first discerned the Sun of Righteousness in the early 2000's in Zurich, Switzerland while ministering at a church that was located on the second floor of a bank building. I have often wondered about the significance of the location. A student noted that she saw a forty-foot being that looked like an angel. Over the years since, I have encountered this being many times, but recently in 2024 and 2025 the Sun of Righteousness is becoming more and more central in our experience.

---

[1] Hill, A. E. (2008). *Malachi: a new translation with introduction and commentary* (Vol. 25D). Yale University Press.

[2] Psalm 21:8–13

[3] Malachi 3:13-15

Chapter Seventeen:
The Sun of Righteousness

Something wonderful happens when the Sun of Righteousness is revealed: She comes with *healing in her wings.*[1] The word 'healing' first occurs in Genesis 20 where we learn that Abraham went to Gerar, which is south of Gaza. He pretended that his wife, Sarah, was his sister and since she was a beautiful woman, King Abimelech decided to take her as his wife; but the Lord would not tolerate that! The King has a dream and was told by the Lord:

> *"Behold, you are a dead man because of the woman whom you have taken, for she is a man's wife."*[2]

Convicted, Abimelech repented of his actions, spoke with Abraham and there was reconciliation. Abraham then asked the Lord to heal Abimelech:

> *So Abraham prayed to God; and God healed Abimelech, his wife, and his female servants. Then they bore children.*[3]

The scripture then clarifies the nature of the healing:

> *...for the LORD had closed up all the wombs of the house of Abimelech because of Sarah, Abraham's wife."*[4]

The Hebrew word for healing is *marpē*. Its Hebrew root appears over sixty times in the Old Testament, and is used regarding human healing:

> It is sometimes translated "physician" (Gen 50:2) ... is also used of the healing and forgiveness of Gentile nations (Isa 19:22; 57:18). A human subject

> is generally the object of the healing (Ex 21:19). Possibly the most significant usage is in I Sam 6:3, "Then you shall be healed"; (Deut 28:27), "of which you cannot be healed." The themes of healing and restoration as connotations of *rāpā'* are combined in the usage of Isa 53:5, "With his stripes we are healed." In many of the occurrences, it is God who causes healing by divine intervention.[5]

The healing that comes is contained in her wings. Often writers will reveal that the 'wing' here is a reference to "the winged sun disc symbol [Egyptian Horus] which is used throughout the ancient near east as a manifestation of the deity's protection.[6] This is not that healing! It is the healing that can only emerge through the power of the Living God.

I would suggest that this is the era of the revelation of the Sun of Righteousness. Rob Gross is the senior pastor of Mountain View Community Church in Aiea, Hawaii. He and I often speak on the phone as the Lord downloads messages to us from spiritual beings. This has happened for many years, in April 2024, the Lord sent the Sun of Righteousness messages of what is soon to occur. It is the promise of future healing:

> April 1, 2024: Many have been waiting, and it has been a great thing. It has been so slow when you are all ready to go but, in the waiting, there is provision for the vision that is sure to come. It is hard not to be bitter, if not angry, but the increase in authority will release the rest of the story, and the increase of authority must be tested. Things will accelerate in 2024, and you will experience the more. The horses are running and shifting you into position. It is all about discipleship, you see, that will release new

liberty. In order for new ground to be taken, there needs to be a new revelation of the new wine skin being formed that will take down the norm. The fruit is out, not in (the church). The Lord has said before that He is going to take you off the floor and shift you into new dimensions of power and grace. The new thing is not of the old, it is the new. It is arising in your midst so open your eyes and see for shoots are coming up from the ground because there is a ground-floor movement of a new breed and a new seed for kingdom advancement and enhancement. It has been slow, that is for sure; but while you have been waiting the Spirit of God has been working. Beware of the pharaohs and the Kings Herod who are lurking and have been sent by the enemy to kill the babies and stave off the new thing. Call forth the commander of the host to thwart this evil plan, for the Lord's vision and purpose will stand. The Lord has shifted and now gifted the new breed with the new seed for kingdom advancement. The vault will open even more as the new breed rises off the floor. Shift your attention, focus like a laser beam, and you will see rivers of liberty flowing in the desert and releasing new growth.

April 29, 2024: The elders around the throne of God have been activated for a time such as this. There is excitement in heaven. Just as Karen Carpenter sang the song, *You've Only Just Begun*, you have only just begun. It is a new season. There is a new season that will defy reason. Get set for a healing outpouring. The door has opened ajar, but the door is not yet fully open. The mindsets and belief systems of the Lord's people must continue to shift for the Lord to release a new level of power for the hour. You have battled well for decades to clean up the people and now you have transitioned from negative territory to positive territory. The miracles, signs and wonders are contained within my people. Like Stephen and Phillip, the Lord will fill them to preform major exploits, but their mindsets must continue to shift to see the lift into the kingdom realm. The door that has opened is the door into the kingdom realm, for the kingdom of God is not a matter of talk but power. The eagles have landed and there is a merging and converging between the thumb and the forefinger, between the apostolic and the prophetic. There is a merging and converging that will work side by side in tandem to affect the miraculous. You have only experienced a drop of the Kingdom realm; you have only experienced a fragment of what the Lord will do. Get ready for an outbreak that will cause great joy, as when Stephen performed signs and miracles and there was great joy in the city of Samaria. Look for confirmation, look for the signs of the eagle. The key has been turned, and ignition has begun. It only takes a spark to get a fire going, for the Holy Spirit will come like a rushing wind and fan the flame into a barn fire and into a forest fire that spreads across the land. The cisterns have been broken open and the glorious oil of the Lord is being poured out. Be encouraged, for the best is yet to come

The Sun of Righteousness will rise with healing in her wings. This promised day of rising has come. The word rise, *zārah*, means 'to rise, come up'.

> [It} is used in three ways. 1) It refers to the breaking forth of the symptoms of leprosy (II Chr 26:19). 2) It is used of the sun as appearing, without specific reference to the diffusion of its light. 3) It is also used in a figurative sense to speak of salvation, light, glory resulting from God's coming into a man's life. The thought is that as the sun appears in the morning without man's effort but nevertheless floods his surroundings with light and dispels the darkness, so the Lord is sovereign in the bestowal of his salvation, which brings light and glory. The term is used twice of God himself appearing to bring salvation (Isa 60:2) and righteousness to his people (Mal 4:2 [H 3:20]). In both cases there is a prophecy concerning the coming of Jesus Christ as Saviour and Lord.[7]

The promise, which at once seemed far off is now here. The burning is occurring; the fire is here.

> *God is not man, that he should lie, or a son of man, that he should change his mind. Has he said, and will he not do it? Or has he spoken, and will he not fulfill it?*[8]

Expect the healing to happen!

---

[1] Translations vary, most using 'its wings' or 'his wings'. Here, she' or 'her' are used because that is the way I discern them. All three are technically correct: Strong's Hebrew1931 הוּא, יא ה [*huw', beyond, Pentateuch), hiy'*/hoo/] pron 3p s. A primitive word; TWOT 480; GK 2085 and 2115; 38 occurrences; AV translates as "that", "him", "same", "this", "he", "which", "who", "such", and "wherein". **1** he, she, it. 1A

himself (with emphasis). 1B resuming subj with emphasis. 1C (with minimum emphasis following predicate). 1D (anticipating subj). 1E (emphasising predicate). 1F that, it (neuter) demons pron. **2** that (with article).[1]

[2] Genesis 20:3

[3] Genesis 20:17

[4] Genesis 20:18

[5] White, W. (1999). 2196 רָפָא. In R. L. Harris, G. L. Archer Jr., & B. K. Waltke (Eds.), *Theological Wordbook of the Old Testament* (electronic ed., p. 857). Moody Press.

[6] Oswalt, J. N. (1999). 1003 כנף. In R. L. Harris, G. L. Archer Jr., & B. K. Waltke (Eds.), *Theological Wordbook of the Old Testament* (electronic ed., pp. 446–447). Moody Press.

[7] (1999). 580 זָרַח. In R. L. Harris, G. L. Archer Jr., & B. K. Waltke (Eds.), *Theological Wordbook of the Old Testament* (electronic ed., pp. 251–252). Moody Press.

[8] Numbers 23:19 ESV

Chapter Eighteen:
Roots and Branches

When the fire comes, Malachi 3 is clear that there will be a purification. However, Malachi 4:1 is more precise. The burning will be so intense that the enemy will be stubble and even more specifically, neither root nor branch will be left:

> The Hebrew word translated stubble is "qash" and refers to the dry, brittle stalks left after grain has been harvested, commonly known as stubble or chaff. In the Bible, it is often used metaphorically to describe something that is insubstantial, easily destroyed, or worthless. The imagery of chaff is frequently employed to contrast the wicked with the righteous, emphasizing the transient and unstable nature of the wicked.[1]

So, what are the roots and branches? This is an important question because the burning that we endure has a purpose, which is to remove the roots and branches. Textually the phrase has its origin in an ancient language and refers to 'son and grandson'.[2] This helps us understand that the roots and branches refer to generational issues. A good start, but what does that mean?

We can add other words to the imagery of the roots and branches – seed, sprout, trees, leaves, fruit. The first biblical mention of trees is in Genesis 2:9, with the predominant ones being the Tree of Life and the Tree of the Knowledge of Good and Evil. The concept of seed (*zera* in Hebrew) comes later in Genesis 3:15:

> *And I will put enmity between you and the woman and between your seed and her Seed.*

> The Hebrew word "*zera*" primarily refers to seed in both a literal and metaphorical sense. Literally, it denotes the seed of plants, as used in agricultural contexts. Metaphorically, it extends to mean offspring or descendants, emphasizing lineage and posterity. This dual usage underscores the concept of continuity and the transmission of life, both physically and spiritually.[3]

More specifically, *zera* can mean 'sperm' and while there is no specific word for 'ovum' in the Hebrew we can conclude that *zera* clearly has generational implications.

Since 2014, the Lord has given us many words about the roots and the branches. The words were given with great enthusiasm and conviction, but the reality was I had no clue what the Lord was trying to say to us.

As has often happened Mimi Lowe gave us the first word on May 17, 2014:

> Don't you know, don't you know, don't you know? It's in the word; dig deeper, you're close, you're close. Go to the Garden of Eden. Go to the beginning. It's in the garden. The trees, the trees, the trees. I've given it to you; I've given it to you.

The next message from the Lord came to me in a dream on my birthday, January 12, 2015. I was looking at an open window and wondered why it was open. There was a brilliant, shinning white branch coming through a hole in the window screen and it was growing very rapidly. Going outside, I saw another branch growing rapidly and I could see my father there. In the ten years since that dream, I have often wondered about the imagery but had not thought to ask myself, "Why did I questioned the open window." In the last few days, the answers have come and Malachi 3:10 holds the answer:

> *"Bring all the tithes into the storehouse,*
> *That there may be food in My house,*
> *And try Me now in this,"*
> *Says the LORD of hosts,*
> *If I will not open for you the windows of heaven*
> *And pour out for you such blessing*
> *That there will not be room enough to receive it."*

In the Old Testament the word 'heaven' is always plural. Therefore, the verse actually says:

> *"I will open the windows of the heavens."*

I like the ESV translation:

> *"... if I will not open the windows of heaven for you and pour down for you a blessing until there is no more need."*

In other words, there will be no more restrictions on the generational blessings from your dad's and/or mom's side. In the dream, I could see my mom on the left side and my dad outside on the right side.[4]

Pondering the branch, I realized a truth: The 'righteous branch' was growing toward the location of both my mom and dad, but it had not reached either of them. Therefore, it had not reached me either. Something had to be dealt with in me before the generational blessings of the Lord would finally be released, first to me and then to my descendants.

I needed the fire to consume the ungodly roots and branches.

Almost one month later, on February 3, 2015, a friend received another word about the branches and roots:

> Will I not, will I not, will I not open the windows of heaven? There's a whirlwind coming of a different sort where the wheat will bow, and the chaff will stand out. Justice and righteousness with peace in the gate will enter into agreement; it's not too late. The lady of justice will no longer stand with the scales of justice and a sword in her hand. Every false witness and those who cheat will find the whirlwind under their feet. Not root nor branch, I say, will be left and I will hide My own in the rock, in the cleft, with eyes to see and ears to hear. My wrath turned away, they no longer fear. The streams have divided; the river runs through and all who are in it will have life anew. So come to Me, run to Me, buy without money. The window will open and pour out a sundry when the root and the branches are in one accord. Grace, grace will come, which but One can afford; the One who paid the price, the One who is Peace. The One who is the Branch and the Tree. Connectors, connectors are needed here. Don't turn away, there is no fear. Go back to what you know, just follow Me and all will become clear on the crystal sea.

Two days later I had this dream

> I was in a forest and realized I needed to get back to my cabin to check out. I followed a dirt road that seemed filled with wood chips, knowing this would take me back to the cabin. At one point the road

went in two directions but then rejoined further up. I could see this as I looked from a distance. I arrived at a warehouse, still following the road. In the warehouse, I looked through two windows on the other side, and on the left saw two cabins. The one to my left was the one I had rented. At my feet I saw some stuff that included gas cans - things that I might have had in the cabin. Then several coat hangers with clothes on them were in my hand. (Had I already removed my stuff from the cabin?). I went to the cabin and there was a caretaker there. He said, "You were to check out at 6am." What? What a ridiculous time! Then he said, "You will owe one thousand times for each minute that you didn't check out. I think it was now around 9:00am then.

It seemed pertinent that there was a forest, windows and wood chips in the dream, but it would be years before I finally understood. Now in retrospect, it's become clear that in the context of this chapter's discussion:

- The forest equates to the trees, roots and branches
- The wood chips illustrate the attempts of the enemy to destroy the righteous roots and branches
- Getting off the correct course is about straying from God's righteous pathway
- The two windows in the warehouse seem to represent the male and female/ father and mother sides of the generational line (left = mother, right = father)
- Since I was renting, I was a debtor
- The gas cans left in the cabin represent a loss of power

- Coat hangers are about the gift of discernment ("Why?" you might ask? Read on.)
- The caretaker is the enemy
- Checkout at 6 AM – completely irrational and inconvenient, which is an enemy tactic
- 1,000 times per minute debt, so 1000 x 180 minutes = an exorbitant cost, which represents the debt created by generational trading that has affected the roots and branches, compromised our blessings and generated curses

I had not understood what the hangers meant in the above dream until about three years later when I had another dream in October 2018. I was holding a clothes hanger with a cottage cheese shirt on it. When I woke up, I understood the dream immediately - discernment moves a person from "milk to solid food,"[5] comparable to the way cottage cheese is a transition from milk to something more solid. During this transitional time, you get the 'hang' of discernment.

At the same time, we experienced a literal sign and wonder. While on a ministry trip to Manhattan, Donna ordered some hangers from Walmart, but they never came. After we arrived home, two boxes of hangers arrived. Then next day more hangers arrived, and day after day more hangers arrived until we'd received 33 boxes of hangers. I made a trip to our local Walmart, hangers in tow. As I stood before the register, telling my story to the clerk, she punched her computer and informed me that they had no record of us ordering any hangers. The following week we had an Academy at Aslan's Place and thirty-three students came! I then distributed a hanger to each student, reminding them that they are going to get the 'hang' of discernment.

In my forest dream there had been hangers with clothes of them. I realized that perhaps the Lord was showing me that through mature discernment - good clothes vs collage cheese clothes - I would gain victory over the generational iniquity.

It is noteworthy during my dream I had arrived at a warehouse, which has now been realized as the home of Mountain View Community Church in Aiea, Hawaii.

In 2019, Donna and I were visiting our daughter, Corrie, and her family in Boulder City, Nevada. It was the night before we were to fly to Cranbrook, Canada and I woke up with a terrible itch. I thought I was under an attack and rebuked everything I could think of to rebuke, but the itching did not cease. The next morning, I told my son-in-law what happened, and he apologized. He had taken a blanket from the room where his daughter's cats stayed and put in on my bed. I am allergic to cats, but the itching was relevant. In Cranbrook, a lady suffering with cancer came for prayer and as I sat next to her my back started itching and I realized that I was discerning the cancer. I remembered a prayer we constructed in Texas some years ago, after which I wrote the following in *Come Up Higher*:

> I was in Dallas, Texas, in January 2006, leading an Advanced Discernment Training and Exploration School, when I had finally taken the itching for as long as I could. I told the school that my back had been itching. Others immediately reported that their backs had been itching too. So, what was this all about? I asked the seers what they were observing, and they saw what looked like a bramble bush on my back. We began a search through the Word of God, trying to understand what

connection a bramble bush might have to issues in our lives and our generational lines. We included all references to bramble bushes, thorns, thistles, and nettles in our search.[6]

As we explored the generational issues, we found there were false belief systems that affected the righteous branches. These systems appeared as parasitic vines, which wrapped around the righteous branches.

2016 exploded with more revelation from Jana Green:

> February: You create your abundance from the things that are. The invisible is yet to be seen. Faith is substance of things that [we] hope for, by a heart that believes. Go back to the branches. Its almond blossom was first. It awakens the heart to what is real. The branches are the connection to what you have always had. For these trees that produce are the youth. The branches are what affects the land, through the windows that are connected to the grid. The access to the windows is where you are unified. Transference of blessings of time by Selah. The grid is protected by the frequency where you start. The DNA will resonate by the sound of the heart. The heart looks through the windows of the grid. The creation is waiting for the sons to be lead. The re-creation is defined from the heart of the original design. Blessings of truth by what you knew. Selah has a way to time and dimensions to change the land. You take back creation from where you stand. From the mountain of Zion is where you were born. The gates are opened by the sons that are known. You are the godly ones who know the mercies of God. To reproduce good fruit by who you were.

March: Connected to the highways of Zion in the unity of heaven from the fire, through and to the fire you were made. Its original design of the DNA was written before paths of time were laid. What was, is and will be. From Him, through Him and to Him, realigned to be free. The roots support the branches and connect you to the life of the tree. The eyes of the heart to be enlightened to the highways of Zion. Remove the path of Chronos; there will be no more delay. Connect the highways of holiness for the price has been paid.

July: There is <u>a sound in the gate</u>. It is the entrance to Zion. We never cease praying for Zion's sake. We never keep silent for this is where the kingdom is made. From the heart within you connect, but you are here because you all expect. This place you enter in will activate your senses for heaven's intention. A caution to <u>guard your heart</u> for creative judgement is rooted in true discernment and offense will lead you into deception. The judgments are made at the gate but for this one there is a way of holy escape. The remnant calls to understand not just the spiritual but the heart of man. <u>And all will be rooted and grounded in love for the purposes on earth are from above.</u> What is it for but not to know the invisible God and His glory to behold? It seems simple but the grid is complex for it is a table set before you where evil is put to the test. All exist in the heart of God, but He looks for the remnant to release His love. The language was made from the original place when all your days were written you were given power and grace. Some know a touch and some know a smell, some hear a sound, and others know of colors to tell. Every dot and tiddle of line to light, to a frequency, to a color; it is time to align. And you are all unique in the way you go. Don't say it is for another for He gave it to you to be bold. <u>And you will cross through to the zeal of the Lord to burn up every root and branch to lay bare the heart of Gold, and it is not just for you.</u> So, learn to carry it well; a generation to heal the sons and daughters will do well. For some it is personal in their church; live by example and do not try to make it work. To another, a torch is given to the nations, even into the darkness, even into the hatred. By faith you enter in and that what pleases God. Don't control the process because He turns it all from a heart of love.

The family tree illustrates a 'tree' with branches connecting one generation to another. But there is a problem; there are two branches coming down the family line. Spiritually, there is a righteous branch, but there is also an unrighteous branch that is choking out the favor and blessings meant to flow down through the righteous branch. This unrighteous branch spawns all kinds of aberrant growth – vicious vines, weeds, spores, fungus, parasites, bacteria and mold. It is a jungle of immense evil that totally corrupts the goodness of our God in our lives.

In 2014, I had a dream about a relative. I was with a couple, and while walking toward their house I passed under a tree. The ends of the tree branches stuck to my back, and I had to pull them off. Later, I found out the man was dealing with pornography, and it was revealed that it was a generational issue coming down his line from his father. I discerned this on my back (the tree stuck to my back). The same day as the dream, I prayed for a man with an addiction to pornography. We discovered that at the age ten, he was in a convenience store and saw pornography for the first time. As we talked, he had a vison of a seed being planted in him, which grew into a tree. His attention was drawn to the tree, and he could see himself trapped in it. After the prayer session, the Lord took him out of the tree cut it down. The Lord had given me an early illustration of what we would discover later.

It is difficult to calculate the enormity of this evil and the impact on every person's life. We only need to go back 25 generations to find over 67 million moms and dads. Each person can initiate evil, which is then deposited in the family line where it corrupts the DNA and RNA of future generations. Worse, this happens time and again over the course of hundreds of generations. Ezekiel 43:7-9 paints a picture of what has happened in the family line:

> *And He said to me, "Son of man, this is the place of My throne and the place of the soles of My feet, where I will dwell in the midst of the children of Israel forever. No more shall the house of Israel defile My holy name, they nor their kings, by their harlotry or with the carcasses of their kings on their high places. When they set their threshold by My threshold, and their doorpost by My doorpost, with a wall between them and Me, they defiled My holy name by the abominations which they committed; therefore I have consumed them in My anger. Now let them put their harlotry and the carcasses of their kings far away from Me, and I will dwell in their midst forever.*

This is an excellent illustration of what is happening with the ungodly branches, which have been laid beside the righteous branch and negated the generational blessings of the Lord. Isaiah actually called Lucifer an abominable branch.

> *But you are cast out of your grave like an abominable branch, like the garment of those who are slain, thrust through with a sword, who go down to the stones of the pit, like a corpse trodden underfoot.*[7]

There is an instability in what the enemy is doing with the DNA and RNA. In Daniel 2:35, Daniel described his vision of the golden statue. Then, Daniel 2:43-44:

> *As you saw iron mixed with ceramic clay, they will mingle with the seed of men; but they will not adhere to one another, just as iron does not mix with clay. And in the days of these kings the God of heaven will set up a kingdom which shall never be destroyed; and the kingdom shall not be left to other people; it shall break in pieces and consume all these kingdoms, and it shall stand forever.*

I would surmise that this difficulty results in all kinds of physical and psychological issues that pass down the generational lines.

One might say, "Well this is all spiritual but what happens in my generational line cannot affect me physically or mentally." But scientific proof is now being explored that dismisses this argument. There is a developing field of DNA and RNA study called Epigenetics, which is the study of changes in gene function that occur without altering the DNA sequence itself, focusing on how environmental and lifestyle factors can influence gene expression and inheritance.[8] One study has shown how the trauma of life is passed down in sperm, affecting the mental health of future generations.

New research shows this is because experiencing trauma leads to changes in the sperm. These changes can cause a man's children to develop bipolar disorder and are so strong they can even influence the man's grandchildren. We were able to demonstrate for the first time that traumatic experiences affect metabolism in the long-term and that these changes are hereditary... acquired traits other than those induced by trauma could also be inherited through similar mechanisms, the researcher suspects.[9]

But this is even more complicated because we are held accountable for every word we speak:

But I say to you that for every idle word men may speak, they will give account of it in the day of judgment. For by your words you will be justified, and by your words you will be condemned.[10]

Death and life are in the power of the tongue, and those who love it will eat its fruits.[11]

All ungodly thoughts and words set up a negative vibration which can affect out body which then can be passed down the family line.[12] This is because every word thought or spoken is registered in the heavens and becomes a legal issue that affects the vibrations of our body, which is then passed down the generational line.

Why does this happen? The problem comes from those in the generational line who have intentionally chosen to not follow the ways of the Lord and keep His commandments; people who deliberately rebelled against the goodness of our God and embraced that which is clearly against the

Lord. Judges 9:7-15 pictures how people have made wrong choices.

> *The trees once went out to anoint a king over them, and they said to the olive tree, 'Reign over us.' But the olive tree said to them, 'Shall I leave my abundance, by which gods and men are honored, and go hold sway over the trees?' And the trees said to the fig tree, 'You come and reign over us.' But the fig tree said to them, 'Shall I leave my sweetness and my good fruit and go hold sway over the trees?' And the trees said to the vine, 'You come and reign over us.' But the vine said to them, 'Shall I leave my wine that cheers God and men and go hold sway over the trees?' Then all the trees said to the bramble, 'You come and reign over us.' And the bramble said to the trees, 'If in good faith you are anointing me king over you, then come and take refuge in my shade, but if not, let fire come out of the bramble and devour the cedars of Lebanon.*

The people had chosen a bramble, a thorn, a nonproductive unhealthy tree over a healthy and life-giving tree.

Since the beginning of my intense deliverance that began on May 30, 2020, I have often wondered why it was taking so long. As of this writing, it has now been almost 5 years, - 1750 days and counting. The recent intensity of the deliverance has increased to the point that I feel it all day and all night. I can still feel the removal of the roots and branches. Now I finally understand - the depth of evil generated over the centuries in my family line is beyond calculation.

Once the roots and branches are burned up, what happens next? We know from Malachi 4:2 that there is healing and freedom, but the revelation is limited to the Old Testament paradigm. Some 400 years later, Jesus would come as the physical manifestation of the true BRANCH.[13] He would die on the cross and His resurrection would make a way through His blood for the final removal - the burning up of the ungodly roots and branches. At salvation, we are then rooted into Him.[14] He is the true vine, and we become His branches.[15]

We need to be reconnected to the original design that Elohim intended. We need to be reconnected to the Tree of Life and allow those branches to flow down through our generational line.

Jana Green had this word in 2019:

> Though it was in the garden, in the midst there was a tree of life, and all your days were connected to realign to the path of life. For in life, you learn wisdom and in wisdom you know truth. For the fruit of righteousness is the tree of life and the tree of life is your proof. This is why it is important to access the gates for this leads to the heart of the garden where the tree of life is grace.
>
> The inheritance is sure for it is written in the book. To abide with the tree of life is to keep you aligned through his grace and truth. Fruitfulness is abundance if your eye is open to see, for the tree of life roots are in the original self and my presence is the fruit that you see.

True life flows from this righteous origin. We must do our part to see that our descendants receive from us a true connection to the origin of the Tree of Life and the BRANCH. We are instructed to guard our hearts with all diligence for from it flows the springs of life.[16] Unfortunately, the heart is still deceitful and desperately wicked which perpetuates the growth of the ungodly branches in the family line. But we can make the decision to stop this wickedness in our lives and see righteousness perpetuated in our line.[17]

Direction for our lives is given in Psalm 1 - we are to be mature trees planted by the river of God, the River of Life. The contrast between the righteous branch and the unrighteous branch is startling:

> *What delight comes to those who follow God's ways! They won't walk in step with the wicked, nor share the sinner's way, nor be found sitting in the scorner's seat. Their pleasure and passion is remaining true to the Word of "I Am," meditating day and night in his true revelation of light. They will be standing firm like a flourishing tree planted by God's design, deeply rooted by the brooks of bliss, bearing fruit in every season of their lives. They are never dry, never fainting, ever blessed, ever prosperous. But how different are the wicked. All they are is dust in the wind—driven away to destruction! The wicked will not endure the day of judgment, for God will not defend them. Nothing they do will succeed or endure for long, for they have no part with those who walk in truth. But how different it is for the righteous! The Lord embraces their paths as they move forward while the way of the wicked lead only to doom.*[18]

---

[1]https://biblehub.com/hebrew/7179.htm

[2] https://tips.translation.bible/story/translation-commentary-on-malachi-41/zechariah 4 – olive and branches

[3] https://biblehub.com/hebrew/2233.htm

[4] The Lord has revealed to us this is how we can tell which side of the family tree to focus, the mom side is on the left of our body and the father's side is on the right side.

[5] Hebrews 5:14

[6] *Come Up Higher*. Chapter 25

[7] Isaiah 14:19

[8] https://pmc.ncbi.nlm.nih.gov/articles/PMC2791696/#:~:text=Epigenetics%20has%20been%20defined%20and,a%20change%20in%20DNA%20sequence.

[9] https://centralfasd.org/how-the-trauma-of-life-is-passed-down-in-sperm-affecting-the-mental-health-of-future-generations/

[10] Matthew 12:36–37

[11] Proverbs 18:21

[12] https://aslansplace.com/language/en/the-sound-of-the-lord-paul-l-cox/. See also *Molecules Of Emotion: The Science Behind Mind-Body Medicine by Candace Pert*.

[13] Zechariah 6:12, Isaiah 11:1, Jeremiah 23:5, Jeremiah 33:15

[14] Ephesians 3:17, Colossians 2:17

[15] John 15:1-17

[16] Proverbs 4:23

[17] The state motto of Hawaii is "The Life of the Land is Perpetuated in Righteousness."

[18] Ps 1:1–6 TPT

CHAPTER NINETEEN:
BRANCHES AS BELIEF SYSTEMS

I do not know when the thought occurred to me, so profound that I knew it must be from the Lord. Visually, in the Spirit it resembles what we might look like - trees and branches. Note Mark 8:24:

> *And he looked up and said, "I see men like trees, walking."*

But there was a second part to the thought. Seeds, roots, trees, branches and leaves can be interpreted as belief systems, which seems to make sense. Going back to the beginning in the Garden of Eden, there were two trees – the Tree of Life, and the Tree of the Knowledge of Good and Evil. The Tree of Life is the righteous belief system and in Proverbs we are told that Wisdom is the Tree of Life.[1] The Tree of the Knowledge of Good and Evil is the unrighteous belief system. Both systems 'branch out' down the family line. I could easily confirm this all seems logical and makes sense, but I am a man of the Word, so does the Bible actually support this view? Yes, it does.

Look at Matthew 12:33–37:

> *Either make the tree good and its fruit good, or else make the tree bad and its fruit bad; for a tree is known by its fruit. Brood of vipers! How can you, being evil, speak good things? For out of the abundance of the heart the mouth speaks. A good man out of the good treasure of his heart brings forth good things, and an evil man out of the evil treasure brings forth evil things. But I say to you*

that for every idle word men may speak, they will give account of it in the day of judgment. For by your words you will be justified, and by your words you will be condemned.

Words originate in our belief systems. If our belief system is not from the Tree of Life, then unrighteous thoughts are conceived and are expressed in evil words, which then give birth to ungodly roots, trees and branches that are passed down from generation to generation.

Jeremiah 17:7 paints a vivid picture of this reality:

Blessed is the man who trusts in the LORD, and whose hope is the LORD.

For he shall be like a tree planted by the waters, which spreads out its roots by the river,

And will not fear when heat comes;

But its leaf will be green,

And will not be anxious in the year of drought,

Nor will cease from yielding fruit.

The heart is deceitful above all things,

And desperately wicked; Who can know it?

I, the LORD, search the heart, I test the mind,

Even to give every man according to his ways,

According to the fruit of his doings.

Much can be written about the power of the tongue and its destructive force in our lives as the expressions of evil thoughts and words flow down through countless generations of ungodly belief systems. We have not paid attention to the reality of the power of words in our lives. We should be stunned by another verse in Proverbs 18:21:

> *Death and life <u>are</u> in the power of the tongue, and those who love it will eat its fruit.*

I had asked the Lord to verify that He was indeed leading us to contend for healing at Mountain View Community Church in Aiea, Hawaii. Out of that concern we planned and held a two-night Healing Encounter event at the church. On Saturday, the second night, I was standing in the front and discerned the Tree of Life. As I placed my hands on the Tree, I could feel the leaves and a thought suddenly invaded my mind:

> The Tree of Life is a belief system.
>
> Jesus is the BRANCH.
>
> The BRANCH is the mind of Christ, the correct belief system.
>
> The Holy Spirit is Wisdom and is the Tree of Life.
>
> The leaves are 'words' that flow from the righteous belief system.
>
> The leaves are 'the words', which are for the healing of the family.

The Pure Word translation of the New Testament clarifies the Greek word translated 'nation' in Revelation 22:2:

> *In the middle of its Street and on either side of the river, from there on either side a Tree of Life, yielding twelves fruits according to each month, yielding its fruit one to every person and the leafs of the Tree for household health of the nations.*

In Colossians 2:6-9, Paul draws on the concept of roots to express how we must not concentrate on ungodly belief systems of the world:

> *As you therefore have received Christ Jesus the Lord, so walk in Him, rooted and built up in Him and established in the faith, as you have been taught, abounding in it with thanksgiving. Beware lest anyone cheat you through philosophy and empty deceit, according to the tradition of men, according to the basic principles of the world, and not according to Christ. For in Him dwells all the fullness of the Godhead bodily."*

Psalm 1:1-3 also clearly draws an analogy regarding the wisdom of righteous over unrighteous counsel and trees:

> *Blessed is the man*
> *Who walks not in the counsel of the ungodly,*
> *Nor stands in the path of sinners,*
> *Nor sits in the seat of the scornful;*
> *But his delight is in the law of the LORD,*
> *And in His law he meditates day and night.*
> *He shall be like a tree*
> *Planted by the rivers of water,*
> *That brings forth its fruit in its season,*
> *Whose leaf also shall not wither;*
> *And whatever he does shall prosper.*

Jana Green was a forerunner in understanding that the original intent of the Lord was that He would be the seed, root and branch that would grow through the generations, releasing the correct belief system. She prophesied in 2018:

> This is about the branch, the true root for the Tree of Life. This is the mountain of the Lord, for the earth will be filled with the knowledge of the Lord as the water covers the sea. You are pushing against what

hasn't been touched before, but I have made a way for the knowledge of the Lord. There is more to my word than first perceived. Now, deeper still till the heart believes. Trust in the Lord with all your heart for your understanding is being renewed to acknowledge and take part. Let your heart hold fast to my word. Wisdom will lead out, for the regeneration is here. In all your ways acknowledge Him. Let his righteousness be known but when you align the path will grow brighter to the full light of day. Like Enoch, His glory will be known. Watch over your heart with all diligence for from it flows the spring of life. Let your gaze be fixed like flint for the eyes of the Lord are on you and you are His delight. Now, this is important - to acknowledge the mountain of the Lord for clean hands and a pure heart and for more revelation to be made known. If the roots are holy the whole tree is holy for when it comes to the original self you are always connected to the Lord for the regeneration again is here.

---

[1] Proverbs 3:18

CHAPTER TWENTY:
A TESTIMONY: ROOTS & BRANCHES – THE BEGINNING

I must begin by honoring the restorative nature of Jesus Christ, and of Aslan's place. When God decides to do something new on the earth, religion and those bound by it, shun the new and therefore making it challenging for them to Pioneer. Jesus was a Pioneer of what the Father wanted to do, as we must die to self the same way. I'm grateful that Aslan's Place has chosen to move forward boldly, making my process a little smoother. I must give honor where honor is due. Though it may be a road less traveled, to forerun it is necessary to bring in the new. People are hurting and suffering and Jesus is the answer. We should always welcome in any way he wants to do it, even if its unfamiliar to us, as we lay down our own understanding for His.

Now let's begin to unpack how the roots and branches appeared in my life. I would have to repeat it as the Lord said it to me, He was resurrecting me. Which I know has many complexities in our natural mind, but easy for the Lord. As Paul would say Philippians 3:10 to know Jesus and the power of his resurrection. Do I understand everything there is about the roots and branches? No, but I do know that they have been instrumental in my resurrection process. As time goes by, I am sure the Lord will unpack more revelation. But we walk by faith and not by sight.

If I only went by my understanding, I would have quit a long time of go, His understanding was more important to me. I just had finished taking Billy Graham's school of evangelism and cried all the way through it, the anointing was so strong on it. I soon begin to seek the Lord cry out day and night for the Lord to send me to nations to bring people into his kingdom. I kept before him day and night to see where he would send me to win souls for him. I would not relent because I could just see all the souls that needed to be saved. Religion teaches you to do for the Lord, but Jesus is not religion, he is about restoration. The Lord spoke to me after a few days, and it almost seemed audibly. These words pierced my spirit, what kind of God would I be if I healed the nations and didn't heal you. Wow, that was not the answer I was expecting. Little did I know this started a five-year journey of continuous deliverance twenty-four hours a day and much inner healing that took place because of those words.

Obviously, this is a long story and may come out in a book one day, there is much to share about the God who restores, and the process, but I am focusing on the roots and branches right now. I am getting there, just follow me on this grand adventure with our amazing God. The roots and branches were the third stage of my healing process when they manifested. Let's start with a few details that lead to the roots and branches appearing. I would lay in bed and the Lord would start pouring into my right hand an inner healing anointing that was binding up my wounds. I could feel puss pockets of neglect come out like chunks afterward and many other things just poured out of me as the Lord was doing Isaiah 61:1 He was healing my broken heart. This process took some time and was very painful, but it was worth it. There was fire that would come on from time to time in this process, which was probably the fire of purification. It would last hours at a time and would come and go.

Next began what seemed like stage two of my healing process, if was very strange and many prophetic people would see in the dimensions what was going on. I would feel a needle threading and sowing into my heart day and night. It was so wild, and the time I had no frame of reference for it, but since it was happening to me I had to keep inquiring of the Lord about it. At times it was painful when the needle went in. Some described the needle they had seen as the color of the cross, and every thread I could see, and feel was red the color of the blood of Jesus. This went on for an entire year. I continued to inquire of the Lord for the scripture of what he was doing to me, because I was always wanting to see the truth of His word as I was experiencing it. I knew the Lord would provide that because that's who He is. This started around February 2019 and went on for a year, with the Lord hemming me in with this needle and thread. Obviously, He did not ask for my permission nor needed to, but this process seemed new with inner healing, and I had not heard of anyone talk about this before. It was tactile and I discerned it around the clock twenty-four hours a day.

He gave me the verse Psalm 139:5 toward the end of the year I finally received the understanding, the Lord himself was hemming me in. No book, no speaker, no one had ever spoke on this, but I knew this was my unique journey with a unique God who did not need my permission to do anything. Again, this was a process, there were many battles that had to be won, many ups and downs in the process, and many tests I had to pass by the grace of God, the Lord held me. He was faithful to me and the process of my restoration even though it was unique.

Next the **roots and branches** started showing up. I must admit my mind was really surprised at the new process. I thought this is very different, what in the world could this be? I knew this was Lord and the Holy spirit was removing these roots and branches. They had begun unwrapping around my body day and night. It started after the needle and thread was over which was about February 2020 and still continues today day and night. Little did I know that Paul had some experiences with the roots and branches and had also discerned them. That was a relief to me, sometimes when you're discerning and experiencing something new it's refreshing to see that others may have some similar experiences, so you can gleam from one another. That is one reason I am writing this, in hopes that if you are experiencing new things with the Lord to trust the process even if it's different.

As the **roots and branches** continue to come out continuously I since the Lord is removing realms and dimensions in the bloodline, restoring me back to original design that He had laid out for me. Again, it's a process and a journey that I am walking with the Lord thru it. An uncommon journey, but a necessary one. Assuming the Lord is removing every root and branch from my generational line that does not bear fruit in me according to John 15:2, so that I can bear His fruit. Seems like endurance is key to the process of restoration.

April Stutzman

Chapter Twenty-One:
Free as a Calf

There is a wondrous consequence of the burning and the healing – freedom!

> *But for you who stand in awe at the sound of my name, a new dawn is coming. For the sun of righteousness will rise with healing in its wings. And you will be free and leap for joy like calves released from the stall.*[1]

Malachi draws on a rare Hebrew word, *pwš*, which has rich imagery:

> The word conveys a sense of carefree and energetic playfulness characteristic of tethered calves released to pasture.[2]

> The image depicted by the simile is that of well-fed calves, suggesting the prosperity of divine blessing. The portrayal in Malachi is one of carefree playfulness indicating peace and security.[3]

I am reminded of a verse in Job 36:16 (NIV):

> *He is wooing you from the jaws of distress to a spacious place free from restriction, to the comfort of your table laden with choice food.*

The unbeliever is secure in the fact that he is the one who is truly free, but that is deluded thinking. One who is not set free by Jesus Christ is a slave to the many innumerable, complex issues of one's life, generations past and environment. An encounter with the furnace and the Sun of

Righteousness at the direction of the risen Savior is the only solution to the confinements of the invisible 'stall' of one's slavery.

> *Therefore if the Son makes you free, you shall be free indeed.*[4]

I have witnessed the freedom from the misery of this stench of this 'stall' confinement hundreds of times in prayer ministry. I have also heard the naysayers rebuke me for believing in such a ministry of freedom as they insist that Christians do not need this because they are already free.

I would ask them, "What is your solution to the pain, misery, sadness, anxiety, depression, etc. of the pew sitters in the local church?" I can hear their responses, "You need to go to church more often, you need to read your Bible more, and you need to pray more." I would also ask, "And how is that working for you?" Sadly, our churches are full of praying, Bible-studying Christians who are still victims of all manner of dysfunction. On top of that, they are often made to feel guilty because the things they are faithfully doing all the recommended activities but are still suffering. The bottom line is that our righteous actions to not set us free – Jesus does.

Once you have received Jesus as your Savior, He who has begun a good work in you continues to dig deep into your spirit, soul and body to bring complete freedom in your life.

Be encouraged and inspired to yield to the refining fire of His desire to set you free by the following testimony:

> Just thought I would take a moment to share with you how things have been going after my prayer session. Since that time, I have had a deep abiding peace that hasn't left, and most of the mental torture

> I have been going through for years has melted away.
>
> It seems so different not to be battling the awful opposition I endured. Now I expect the same terrible feelings to come back or plague me, but they are gone. During the prayer I felt nothing significant but later realized that deep generational strongholds had been released from me.
>
> So, I am very thankful to The Lord and for the strong discernment and deliverance gift that has been entrusted to you. Thank you for serving the Lord and others for His glory.

In essence, generational prayers[5] remove the legal ground of the enemy that enables him to harass you and to steal, kill and destroy things in your life - no more shadow boxing! As a result, one can move freely to do the will of God, unhindered by the enemy because there is nothing of his left in us that he can legally use against us. Hallelujah! This is huge!!

This is a great place to be! If we can dare to change our circumstances by doing these renunciations, we become proactive in partnership with God, taking the next step to get out of where we have been in our past. We move into warp drive to reach the next level with Him! Then, it's on to His destiny for us!

We are saying, "Enough is Enough!" to the enemy of our souls! "Enough is Enough!" to the tormentor! Both personally and generationally, we close doors to the past and to circumstances we may never fully understand or even identify specifically; but things that have impacted our lives negatively, especially if we are stuck somewhere with no clear direction! Through this process, most come to a place of freedom in which they can enjoy their God-given destiny, even if they'd previously been at war with it.

Another Testimony:

> The ministry of Aslan's Place has been immeasurably precious to me. It has bumped my life to a higher dimension and my understanding to have the vision for a much higher walk with our Lord Jesus.
>
> My one hour and three hours of generational ministry with the Prayer Minister has done much for my health and awareness of what I can be for the Lord and as ministry. I want more time to resolve more health and life issues. I desire to 'go on to perfection' and am preparing for more.

Testimony regarding the Ruling and Reigning Prayer:

> For most of my life I have one dream that I hate…it is of dark basements and murky water standing on the floor…and as I walk through the rooms, I realize that there are more and more 'secret rooms'…all dark. In my mind, this is pretty much what was uncovered yesterday in our session. As I came to the last two paragraphs of the Ruling and Reigning Prayer it was like someone switched on a light (from my left peripheral vision) and for the first time in the session my entire face became 'cool instead of flushed'. This morning, I am looking out on my patio and instead of black crows-there are 7 beautiful Robins, so full of life. It just brings tears to my eyes and heart.

God bless you all at Aslan's Place. My greatest desire would be to minister this type of 'setting the captives free' to younger women so they don't have to wait until they are 67 years old. What amazes me is how 'deep my love is for my Lord', yet all of this generational iniquity lurked there. When I really became aware of this (after reading almost every book and seeing every teaching Dr. Cox has done) is to see so many of my health issues and insecurities coming to the forefront in my child. Whatever I must do to cut these ties to my bloodline…I will do for generations now and those to come. Much love and appreciation.

His fire is ready to consume the roots and branches of generations of anguish that have unmercifully plummeted your very being. What keeps you from being all that He intends you to be? Freedom awaits those who yield to the fire.

---

[1] Malachi 4:2 TPT

[2] Hill, A. E. (2008). *Malachi: a new translation with introduction and commentary* (Vol. 25D, p. 352). Yale University Press.

[3] Hill, A. E. (2008). *Malachi: a new translation with introduction and commentary* (Vol. 25D, p. 353). Yale University Press.

[4] John 8:36

[5] Prayers are available free at aslansplace.com or available for purchase electronically or as a hard copy. For more information see: https://aslansplace.com/language/en/product/generational-prayers-2022/

CHAPTER TWENTY-TWO:
THE PLOWMAN

A couple of years ago my daughter, Christy, our office manager called and said that there is this man who keeps giving unusual amounts of money, sometimes only cents but occasionally hundreds of dollars. She sent me a printout of the donations. As I studied the amounts given, I had the thought that the gifts were prophetic. As we tracked the dates and amounts, we were excited to see that very often they were scripture references. The Lord was speaking to us through these donations. One time in Hawaii the Lord told us to set up a model of the tabernacle at the Mountain View Community Church in Aiea, Hawaii, so we did. That Sunday afternoon I received notice of another gift, and the amount was a reference to a passage in 1 Samuel that read, "And they set up the tabernacle in the desert." How was it possible that the person who gave that amount knew?

Another gift shocked me. It was a Sunday morning and Donna had just left her bed when she stepped in some dog urine, slipped and fell. Immediately, I took her to Kaiser's urgent care, expecting at least a five-hour wait. But then, waiting in a line of only one other person, I told the triage nurse whose name was **Grace** what had happened. She told her to go right to x-ray. No line! Afterward, we were instructed to go to the waiting room, which was now filled with over 30 people, and I knew it would be a long wait. We were just seated when a nurse called out Donna' name and I looked to see if another Donna stood up. No other Donna! We entered the doctors' offices and were told to wait for the doctor. Less than a minute later, he entered, looked at the x-ray and said, I am sending you to the casting department for a cast of your wrist. As Donna was being treated, I looked at my phone and another gift had just arrived. It was $54.17, which immediately brought to mind Isaiah 54:17, "No weapon formed against you will prosper." How did he know? [1]

While writing this book, a friend called and asked if I knew the meaning of the 'craftsmen' of Zechariah 1:18-21:

> *Then I raised my eyes and looked, and there were four horns. And I said to the angel who talked with me, "What are these?" So he answered me, "These are the horns that have scattered Judah, Israel, and Jerusalem." Then the LORD showed me four craftsmen. And I said, "What are these coming to do?" So he said, "These are the horns that scattered Judah, so that no one could lift up his head; but the craftsmen are coming to terrify them, to cast out the horns of the nations that lifted up their horn against the land of Judah to scatter it."*

As I read the passage, I realized I had no comprehension of the identity of these craftsmen. My spirit was quickened, and I thought, "These craftsmen seemed very similar to the 'engraver' in Isaiah 54. And yes, it is the same Hebrew word, *harash*. A burst of revelation flooded over me. More insights about the 'burning' was coming.

Let's dissect Isaiah 54:16-17:

> *Behold, I have created the blacksmith who blows the coals in the fire, who brings forth an instrument for his work; and I have created the spoiler to destroy. No weapon formed against you shall prosper, and every tongue which rises against you in judgment, you shall condemn. This is the heritage*

of the servants of the LORD, and their righteousness is from Me," says the LORD.

The Passion Translation expands our understanding of this passage:

See, I am the one who created the craftsman who fans the coals into a fire and forges a weapon fit for its purpose.

There seem to be two spiritual beings involved in the process – a craftsman and destroyer. Note what the engraver does: he fans the coals into a 'fire' and forges a weapon for his work.

The Hebrew word, *ḥāraš* is translated into English as *"engrave, plow, devise."* In Jonah 4:8, a derivative of haras, *harsh* is used. While the meaning of *harsh* is uncertain, it is translated in the English Standard version is *"scorching."*[2]

This idea of heat is clearing implied with the word *haras*, *"engrave."*[3]

To engrave metal requires a temperature of 1800 degrees Fahrenheit.

Then a friend texted me and said this word, *haras,* is used in Psalm 129:

"Many a time they have afflicted me from my youth,"

Let Israel now say —

"Many a time they have afflicted me from my youth;

Yet they have not prevailed against me.

The plowers plowed on my back;
They made their furrows long."
The LORD is righteous; He has cut in pieces the cords of the wicked.
Let all those who hate Zion
Be put to shame and turned back.
Let them be as the grass on the housetops,
Which withers before it grows up,
With which the reaper does not fill his hand,
Nor he who binds sheaves, his arms.
Neither let those who pass by them say,
"The blessing of the LORD be upon you;
We bless you in the name of the LORD!"

The psalmist initiates this song with a reality of their existence – they are afflicted. The Hebrew for the English word afflicted is *ṣārar*, which can be translated as *narrow, tight, distress, straits, suffer distress*. The distress has come from the nations, the generational issues. How has the Lord dealt with this misery? He has sent the plowmen, the craftsmen, the *haras*. They have plowed "my back." This has been my experience! I could feel the rippling of this ferocious, infernal, unquenchable fire burrowing channels on my back.

As you examine Isaiah 54, one can see why the Lord is sending the engraver. The people are in misery, shame and disgrace;[4] afflicted, storm-tossed and not comforted.[5] A solution is needed, and the engraver and destroyer are the solution.

It seems the engraver works in tandem with the destroyer.

> **Behold, I have created the blacksmith who blows the coals in the fire, who brings forth an instrument for his work; and I have created the spoiler [destroyer] to destroy.**[6]

The Hebrew word translated as destroyer is *mašḥît*. It is the same word for the destroyer in Exodus 12:31 when the Lord sent the destroyer against the Egyptians at the time of the Passover.

It seemed the Hebrew word group, *ḥāraš*, had keys to unlocking an understanding of what has been happening to me. Toward the end of the intense burning period of my life, I called Rob Gross on December 4, 2024, and related to him that I was discerning an archangel with a message, which was that the Lord is going to deal with the false prophetic in 2025. That night I sensed a sudden, severe increase in deliverance from my family line. As I sought the Lord about what was happening, I could feel the false prophetic being removed from both sides of my generational line. It was intense witchcraft, and what followed was beyond weird.

The skin all over my body erupted with sores. At first, I thought they were shingles but discovered that shingles are usually located on only one part of the body. By the end of December, I had various kinds of sores all over my body. My back was like a washboard. The itching was terrible, and I spent many hours scratching. I knew through discernment that this was tied to deliverance, but how was it possible for my skin to react so violently to the removal of the enemy from my family line? The intensity of the deliverance eased up by the beginning of January 2025, but with the discovery of a new layer of evil in an Ephesians class the deliverance intensified to a horrible new level of itching. The Lord had exposed new entities, the forces of wickedness in the heavenly places.[7] By the next Ephesians class, others reported that they were also itching, with some experiencing sores on their bodies as well. Why was this happening and how was it tied to the burning? I was not prepared for the revelation that would take place!

By March 2025, my excavation of the Hebrew engraver, *haras*, had unearthed a subterranean treasure trove of understanding. There are many Hebrew words in this word group, one of which is *heres*, meaning sun or irritant. It is an unusual noun for the sun and seems to indicate an exposure to a source of heat. Another meaning is tied to 'burning'. But wait; there is more. *Heres* is also a noun, which denotes an eruptive disease characterized by an itchy skin irritation. Could this reveal an ungodly engraver that the righteous engraver comes against? The verb in this group is *haras and* means to scratch of lacerate and could indicate a deletion of bad information. The verb *'harash I'* means to engrave or to cut into something.[8] How strange! Would this help us understand how the itching through the power of the engraver removes bad information from our family line, i.e. burning up of the roots and branches?

Why did the Lord send these craftsmen, the plowers, the engravers? This is the good news! First, our enemies are eliminated, as revealed in Psalm 129 (TPT) reveals the grandeur of our freedom:

> ***But no matter what, the Lord is good to us. He is a righteous God who stood to defend us, breaking the chains of the evil ones that bound us.***

Second, the freedom that comes from the clash between the engravers and the enemy is so dramatic that no weapon formed against us can ever prosper and we are taken from this horrible place of distress:

> *He is wooing you from the jaws of distress to a spacious place free from restriction, to the comfort of your table laden with choice food.*[9]

That is why the penman of the Song of Songs writes:

> *Rivers of pain and persecution will never extinguish this flame. Endless floods will be unable to quench this raging fire that burns within you. Everything will be consumed. It will stop at nothing as you yield everything to this furious fire <u>until it won't even seem to you like a sacrifice anymore.</u>* [10]

---

[1] After a very long time the Lord gave me permission to contact the one who had given all those gifts. I asked if he knew the meaning of the gifts. He said, "No."

[2] Wood, L. J. (1999). 760 חָרֵשׁ. In R. L. Harris, G. L. Archer Jr., & B. K. Waltke (Eds.), *Theological Wordbook of the Old Testament* (electronic ed., p. 327). Moody Press.

[3] Coppes, L. J. (1999). 759 חרשׁ. In R. L. Harris, G. L. Archer Jr., & B. K. Waltke (Eds.), *Theological Wordbook of the Old Testament* (electronic ed., pp. 327–328). Moody Press.

[4] Isaiah 54:4

[5] Isaiah 54:11

[6] Isaiah 54:16

[7] Ephesians 6:12

[8] https://www.abarim-publications.com/Meaning/Heres.html

[9] Job 36:16 NIV

[10] *The Passion Translation* (B. Simmons, trans.; So 8:7). (2017). BroadStreet Publishing.

Chapter Twenty-Three:
The Bridegroom's Passion

The burning had now lasted for exactly two years, over which I had searched for evidence of others who were experiencing this kind of burning. No results. I even tried to find historical evidence of those who had encountered this tremendous force of our God. Again, no results. As I continued ministering in generational prayer sessions, Aslan's Place interns would join me in person and via Zoom for prayer sessions. Finally, during a prayer time on August 8, 2024, I was sharing with a client and some interns my fire experiences and was startled to hear what an intern from Texas expressed. She had also been burning for almost two years, and she recommended that I look at Song of Songs 8:6-7 in The Passion Translation. I did, and the Lord revealed the underlying treasure in the misery of the burning:

> *Fasten me upon your heart as <u>a seal of fire</u> forevermore.*
>
> *This living, <u>consuming flame</u> will seal you as my prisoner of love.*
>
> *My passion is stronger than the chains of death and the grave, all consuming as the very <u>flashes of fire</u> from <u>the burning heart of God.</u>*
>
> *Place <u>this fierce, unrelenting fire</u> over your entire being.*
>
> *Rivers of pain and persecution will never extinguish this <u>flame.</u>*
>
> *Endless floods will be unable to quench <u>this raging fire that burns</u> within you.*

Everything will be consumed.

It will stop at nothing as you yield everything to <u>this furious fire</u> until it won't even seem to you like a sacrifice anymore.

The imagery is worth examining, using <u>underlined</u> phrases above:

Fasten me upon your heart as <u>a seal of fire</u> forevermore.

The speaker requests to be placed "like a seal upon your heart, as a seal upon your arm," emphasizing the strength and intensity of love, comparing it to fire and stating "for love is as strong as death" and "its flames are flames of fire, a most vehement flame"[1] [Note that a wax seal was made with "hot" wax.]

… all consuming as the very <u>flashes of fire</u>.

The Hebrew word for "flashes" is *rešep*. It is defined "Arrow, burning coal, burning heat, spark, hot thunderbolt, fever."[2] "fire" is *ʾesh* and means physical fire.

…from <u>the burning heart of God</u>

"The Hebrew word "shalhebeth" refers to a flame or blaze, often used metaphorically to describe intense passion or fervor. In the context of the Bible, it can symbolize the consuming nature of love or divine presence." [3]

Brian Simmons wrote as a footnote to Song of Songs 8:6:

> The phase in Hebrew is 'a most vehement flame' and is actually two Hebrew words. The fire is 'a mighty flash of fire,' and the second *'yah,'* which is the sacred name of God himself. The Hebrew *'shalhebet-yah'* could be translated "The Mighty Flame of the Lord Most Passionate."

But what about the strange phase stating, "love is as strong as death"? Joseph Dillon in his book, *Solomon on Sex*, expresses the depth of this phase.

> His love is like death because of its finality and irreversibility. Frequently in the Old Testament, God is presented as jealous in His love for His people, Israel. To say God is jealous simply means he has intense love and concern. He desires Israel's exclusive devotion to Him and not to other gods. In a similar way, true love, says the bride, is like this. It is exclusive and it is intense.[4]

Do we really comprehend the 'fierce' love of our God for us? This love is comparable to the fierce sexual passion of a husband and wife in their marital love. In our modern world one seems to see the Lord as only a taskmaster and one who seems to only want to make our live miserable. How we have underestimated the nature of the *agape* love of God.

There seems to be an order to the burning. For us to know and experience the fierce and all-encompassing passionate fire of the Lord we must first undergo the extinguishing of evil from the past. The roots and branches must be totally consumed so that the depth of His love may be realized. This is the burning.

Following the burning is the 'fusion'."

Nuclear fusion, the process where light atomic nuclei combine to form heavier ones, results in the release of **tremendous amounts of energy**, as seen in the Sun and stars."[5]

This is comparable to the intense love of Elohim towards us. I find it interesting that in Malachi 4, the being is called the 'Sun' of righteousness.

The passionate love of a man for his wife is captured in Johnny Cash's song, *Ring of Fire*. Perhaps it can accurately describe of our Bridegroom's love of His bride, the Church.

> Love is a burning thing
> And it makes a fiery ring
> Bound by wild desire
> I fell into a ring of fire
> I fell into a burning ring of fire
> I went down, down, down and the flames went higher
> And it burns, burns, burns, the ring of fire
> The ring of fire

---

[1] https://www.google.com/search?q=song+of+songs+8%3A6+seal+was+made+of+fire&rlz=1C1ONGR_enUS1005US1005&oq=song+of+songs+8%3A6+seal+was+made+of+fire&gs_lcrp=EgZjaHJvbWUyBggAEEUYOdIBCTEwMDA1ajBq"jealous"M6gCALACAQ&sourceid=chrome&ie=UTF-8

[2] https://www.quotescosmos.com/bible/bible-concordance/H7565.html

[3] https://biblehub.com/hebrew/7957.htm

[4] Dillon, Joseph. Solomon on Sex. Nashville, Tenn: Thomas Nelson Publishers. 1977.

[5] https://www.google.com/search?q=result+of+fusion&rlz=1C1ONGR_enUS1005US1005&oq=result+of+fusion&gs_lcrp=EgZjaHJvbWUyBggAEEUYOdIBCDcwMTNqMGo0qAIAsAIA&sourceid=chrome&ie=UTF-8

Chapter Twenty-Four:
A Sustained Burning

It was probably one of the first Bible verses I memorized as a child yet had no meaning to me. It was a series of words filed away in my brain to recite upon request, standing alone in isolation, out of context and unconnected to any truth before or after this profound language in the book of Romans. It was as if I was walking in the dense fog of Camp Pendleton near Oceanside, CA where I grew up, unable to see in front or behind me.

I held the verse close, yet it was still just a verse. Years later, I explored the list of spiritual gifts that follow and later, as a pastor, I taught the theological truths that precede this verse. The verse itself became a bridge between the theology of Romans 1-12 and the practical Christian living applications that followed.

The verse, Romans 12:1, had a profound effect on my decision to follow the Lord and now, decades after the first memory attempt, I am again revisiting the implications of the Apostle Paul's language.

> *I beseech you therefore, brethren, by the mercies of God, that you present your bodies a living sacrifice, holy, acceptable to God, which is your reasonable service.*

I had never really unpacked what *'a living sacrifice'* meant, and what is a sacrifice anyway?

> A sacrifice in the Old Testament was the manipulation of an animal, vegetal, or liquid as

religious devotion. This can include ritual slaughter, division, reconfiguration, cooking, consuming, and/or complete **burning**."[1]

We are familiar with the story of Abraham and his obedience in offering his son, Isaac as a sacrifice. The altar had been built and the wood laid on the altar because **fire** was going to be put to the wood. The Lord stopped the effort of Abraham and provided a new victim. In this sacrifice, as in all Old Testament sacrifices, the victim was put to death before the sacrifice was completed. The Apostle Paul stunned his readers by urging them, earnestly appealing to them in fact, to do the unthinkable. Place themselves willingly and unconditionally on the burning altar and remain there, constantly burning for the rest of their lives while yielding to His will allowing Him to do whatever He wants with them/us. There was to be no crawling off of the altar when life gets tough.

> The Greek verb for "present" is in the aorist tense, which is used by the writer to present the action of a verb as a "snapshot" event. The verb's action is portrayed simply and in summary fashion without respect to any process,"[2]

Romans 12:1 in The Passion Translation:

> *And live in holiness, experiencing all that delights his heart. For this becomes your genuine expression of worship.*

This is a sobering understanding of what it means to be a disciple of Jesus Christ. You make a final decision in your life, which is to climb up onto the sacrificial altar of the Living God, be ignited by His fire, and forever remain there in a 'sustained burn'.

In a rocket engine a sustained burn refers to the continuous combustion of fuel, producing thrust for a prolonged period, as opposed to a brief or intermittent burn. As a living sacrifice, we are in a sustained burn - a constant state of being empowered through the fuel of the Power of the Living God to accomplish what the Lord desires to do through us. It is our final death to self, our death with Him at the cross, and our being raised up in Christ to live in resurrection Power as He works through us to accomplish His will.

This is:

- Living constantly in the burning bush

- Living at the throne of God, which is surrounded by fire and rests on burning wheels

- Living in the fiery stream which flows from the throne of God

- Living in the fire of holiness where, like Moses, we recognize Who He is and fall in worship at His feet

- Living forever as we follow the pillar of fire to do His will

- A burning desire, an uncontrollable longing, to please our Bridegroom

- A burning passion to express our love and worship of our King

- A burning love that is an intense, all-consuming affection for the Lover of our soul

- A burning need to introduce others to this intense love of our beloved

- A burning curiosity to explore the depths of the wisdom and creation of the One who loves us

- A burning enthusiasm and overflowing excitement to venture into discovery of WHO HE IS AND WHAT HE DOES AND WHAT HE HAS CREATED

THIS IS TO EXPERIENCE THE FURIOUS BURNING LOVE OF OUR BRIDEGROOM

---

[1] Starbuck, S. R. A. (2016). Sacrifice in the Old Testament. In J. D. Barry, D. Bomar, D. R. Brown, R. Klippenstein, D. Mangum, C. Sinclair Wolcott, L. Wentz, E. Ritzema, & W. Widder (Eds.), *The Lexham Bible Dictionary*. Lexham Press.

[2] Heiser, M. S., & Setterholm, V. M. (2013; 2013). *Glossary of Morpho-Syntactic Database Terminology*. Lexham Press.

AFTERWORD

This book was finished, edited and about ready to go to print, but apparently God wasn't finished yet!

"It has to be unto something," was my frequent comment to friends over the last five years of constant deliverance, burning and itching. This sovereign work of the Lord had to be unto something, but along the way I had another thought, a desperate one, "Will all of this ever be over?" Finally, the answer came, "Yes, Paul, it is over."

It was resurrection day, April 20, 2025. I awoke realizing that I was different and the deliverance, burning, and itching was different. Yes, it was over, but I did not tell anyone – not until I could be sure. Day after day I monitored my nights before finally admitting to myself and others that it was over.

The end of all of this coincided with a dramatic shift in our lives. The Lord spoke to us and said we were to move to Hawaii. It was something I never wanted to do! I loved our house in the high desert of Southern California and never intended to leave our amazing home. Moving would mean we would have to sell both our house and the Aslan's Place property, often referred to informally as 'Sagebrush' or 'Sagebrush Ranch'. But I had no doubt - we were to move. And then we became excited about what the Lord is going to do, about the revival that has already started in Hawaii, about the unfulfilled call on our lives.

It is now April 29, 2025. Both properties are already in escrow, and the Lord is blessing us beyond anything we ever could have imagined. We are dreaming of a trip around the United States sharing with others our journey with the 'fire' before moving to Hawaii.

Yes, all of this was unto something! The Lord has burned out much so He can now fill the empty cavity with His Power.

There remains a question for all of those who are called by His name. "Are you now willing to yield to His fire so you can join the company of the 'Burning Ones' who will be a mighty army of end-time soldiers, commanded by the King of Kings and Lord of Lords?" Th is the army that will welcome in the harvest of billions of souls, bring healing from the devastation of generations, and disciple others to serve their King. Will you answer as Isaih did, and as we along with many others have replied?

> *And I heard the voice of the Lord saying, "Whom shall I send, and who will go for us?" Then I said, "Here I am! Send me."*[1]

---

[1] Isaiah 6:8 (TPT)

APPENDIX ONE:
PROPHETIC WORDS OVER THE YEARS

For over 20 years the Lord has been speaking prophetically to us about fire, some of which have previously been shared. Following is a sampling more 'fire words'.[1]

Aug 2005:
Keep the **fire** going. What's coming is bigger than you can imagine… What is your vision? Multiply it by 100s, 1000's. It's too small, get it bigger…They will be sign. Where no berries (technical word for grapes on bush) — sign.

March 2006:
This is part of the **burning bush**

The **fire** will not consume x 3

What I have done

Follow your dreams x 2

I'll show you the way

New things are coming

The new winds are blowing

And I'm breathing upon you

Do you want to come higher?

Do you want to come higher?

Do you want to come higher?

You're invited

I love you, my people

I love you, my bride

And I'm longing for you, for

Every part of you

Every corner of your heart

My joy is going to be like a **fire** x 2

It is going to spread

Uncontrollable

There will be **wildfires** in the desert

That cannot be quenched

That cannot be put out

March 2006:
Fire, fire, fire

Water, water, water

Oil, oil, oil

It's the holy **fire**

It's The living water

It's The sacred oil

August 2006:
… There is a wave going to come through this land. It is not a water wave; it is a wave of **fire**. To some it will be an answer to prayer, ministries born, revitalization. To some it will be devastation.

March 2007:
Fire, fire, fire. The **fire** is falling. The **fire is falling to burn** it all away, and then the glory can come. I am preparing you for the glory. I have to **burn away** all the garbage so the glory can sink in…

August 2007:
I bring you **fire**, mountains of **fire**! You will be purified with

My **fire**! You will be in My Holy Presence. Receive the purification of My **fire**. I am releasing My fire... Allow the purification to take place.

September 2008:
Blowing, blowing. Looks like lifting something out of a well. Spring up out of a well. **Fire. Spark.** Like a **volcano of fire, sparks**. Crying out. Birthing. **Fire, such fire, heat**. Holiness unto the Lord. Holiness unto the Lord...

November 2008:
The **fire** is going to come. The water is going to come. The **fire** and the water are going to flow. There is the **fire** of My spirit here is to consecrate you, to set your path, to be warriors in this land.

January 2009:
There is a *bonfire*. He is putting individuals in a fire. I am turning up the **heat**. It is not a time to be passive. You cannot ignore what is going on... You will be Holy, for I am Holy. The **fire will burn up** everything that is not Holy. He is asking for permission to allow you to put in the **fire**. He is looking at your heart. You must choose this day who you will serve... Will you allow Me to **burn** in you? To **burn** away the flesh. Only the Holy is left. Only the pure. The Lord is looking in the **fire** and He is seeing His face in the gold. If you allow Him to **burn** you, to melt you, then you will see His face in you. His reflection will be in you. It is like gold that is melted. He sees His face in you. No more passivity, no more sitting on the fence. You must **burn** for Me... You must be a **fire** starter. A **fire** carrier. Holy Spirit **fire**.

March 2009:
Whirlwind of **fire**, whirlwind of **fire**, whirlwind of **fire**. Expand, expand, expand, expand. You've never been here

before. Shifting sands, shifting sands, shifting sands. **Chariots of fire, chariots of fire, chariots of fire** to take you higher. Come on board. Take you higher. Explore other dimensions.

April 2009:
Passed over, you have crossed over the divides, you crossed over the Jordan, you have crossed over the promised land. I'm releasing the **fire** of My Holy Spirit… All-consuming **fire, burning**. Spreading from here to the nations. **Fire** of the bonanza. It is going from here, the **fire** is starting from here, a redeeming fire a consuming **fire** to wash away past iniquities. He is wanting to put it inside all those here to make none of us the same. Will you receive the **fire**? … Do not be afraid of man and what he can do and be fearful of me alone because I am the consuming **fire**, it cleanses you and replenishes you. Will you step into My **fire**?

April 2009:
I'll fan them

I'll blow on them

Their **embers to ignite**

Fire for my glory

The **fire** of My might

Fire to burn dross, weeds and dead wood too

Fire to ignite new power in you

Fire to give life to plans not yet birthed

Fire to give growth to what you think has been cursed

This **fire** is good

It gets rid of the old

Giving soil new strength to bring forth life strong and bold

December 2009:
Wind within a wind, wheel within a wheel.

The **fire** is getting brighter, and it is engulfing You.

The **fire** is brighter, understand the sword is sharper, it is two-edged.

The **fire** is blue, but it is white, but it is orange, and it is yellow.

For when one is ending, one is beginning.

The light is shone, refracting within You.

When the **fire** changes, the **fire** changes.

I am the lighter, I am the lamp, I am the flint, I am the wood.

You are the runaway, I am the shelter, and I am Peace.

But do not forget I own the colors, and I own your **fire**…

January 2010:
The fear of the Lord is pure… My **fire** has been released upon the earth and in this region… The **fire** has been stirred, and I am that **fire** within each of you. It is the **fiery stones**. The **fire** is in the **fiery** stones. There is a release. Pick them up and place them in your heart. For they will bring healing to the nations. Nothing can extinguish this **fire**… The **fire** shall spread as you release the stones… The **fiery stones** set the captives free.

July 2010:
A **new fire** is coming, a **revealing fire**; it is aligned with the **all-consuming fire**, It's an **electrical fire of power**. It's clear and unexpected. A **cleansing fire**, a **revival fire** in this hour. It is for the age to come in power.

November 2010:
The birthing of a **fire**

Uncontainable

The Birthing of a **fire**
Unquenchable
Unstoppable

June 2011:
Deeper; go deeper, deeper, deeper…
That's gonna take you higher.
Explore new realms, new realms.
Fire, fire, fire, fire,
Explosion, explosion, baptism, baptism, baptism of love
More power… increase power…

June 2012:
For I am producing and emerging a purer pillar in the House of Aslan and there will be a **fire of holiness**, there will be a **fire of holiness**, a **fire of the fear of God**, growing and growing and growing. And it will be fun in the pillar of the fear of God for perfect love has driven out fear and perfect love is safe and secure but does not tolerate evil…pure hands, clean heart.

July 2012:
This is the **fire** prophesied for the end times. This is the **fire** that will turn and purify and refine My church so that they will go forth in power. You have been through the **fire**. You have said yes to my purification. After the **fire** comes authority. After the purging comes authority. After the **fire** and purging of your words and the understanding of their power comes position…

October 2012:
It looks like the Lord is throwing out the **fire** and it starts to consume everything in front of it. A **holy fire** to cleanse, **burn**. You were created in My image. You were not created

in the image of man. I am sending **My fire, My holy fire** to cleanse to purge that you might be holy as I am holy. **Burn it up. Will you receive my burning, My fire**? Open your hearts. Open your minds. Receive it in the depths of your being for it will cleanse and purge. I am sending **My holy fire** so that you will be prepared to receive more. It is purging the elemental spirits.

May 2013:
The **fire** is going to increase

Don't be afraid of **My holy fire**

Don't' be afraid to come into **My holy fire**

Just as I **burn** off the chaff

I am **burning** things out of you

And I'm replacing it with new…

Continue to receive

February 2014:
The future government is rising. **Fire** is coming. The **fire** is coming. He is coming in the clouds; He is coming in the clouds; He is coming in the clouds. He is making a sound… Awaken, awaken, awaken. Do you feel the rhythm of my glory? He's coming in the clouds, with power and thunder and lightning… Look up! A wave is coming from Hawaii… It's going to touch every mountain, awaken a tsunami to the uttermost parts of the earth.

Feb 2015:
From the west to the east, they will come; from the north to the south, they will run. Take care of the western gate for the eastern gate is open Prepare, prepare, prepare. The time of the Lord is approaching. Prepare, prepare, prepare. It's a new door, a new day, a new life. **Fire** in the sky, look for **fire** in the sky. It signals change for the people of God. Before

there is **fire** on the earth, there is fire in the heaven. The unseen being made seen… Exchange the mind of man for the Spirit of God and then you will see **fire**…

July 2016:
The **fire** is from the inside out. This is the working of the Kingdom of God without a doubt. To **burn** away the dross and the thistles [**Paul feels Truth burning like a fire**]. And if you could face the **fire** it will lead. I will guide you to the unknown, to the hidden place where you believe. For the kingdom of God is within. …

September 2016:
There is **fire** in the house… A new day is coming and what I have for you has already been started. There is **fire** in the house, a **burning** that will overtake many iniquities. **My fire** is in the house. **My fire** is in the house. Death has not overtaken you and evil has to go…

Jan 2017:
The **fiery ones** are burning. The **fire** is on the throne and the **fire** is in the House of God again. There will come a returning in your nation like your ancestors did a long time ago. The **fiery ones** are going out. Chariots and horses. Activity is rising. The **fire is burning**. There are myriads of angelic forces, chariots, horses and they are waiting to be released. It is starting in your nation, but it is going to be a network around the globe even places you haven't explored yet. There is going to be healing and revival in many places. Keep the fire burning…

November 2017:
You have stepped over a threshold into a new dimension

There is big responsibility with this

You are being called to a deeper, deeper commitment

To whom much is given much is required

I am aligning you to the things that I purposed you for to the destinies I called you into

Fire, more fire; more fire is coming to burn those things in life that have been holding you back, keeping you from seeking, keeping you from moving into destiny pathways, seasons, relationships…

May 2018:

It's time to awaken. It's time for the awakening of the pioneers of the realm of my domain and dominion. I am sending **fire** of awakening. Yeah, to **burn** away the dross and it's not a coin toss that tries to trade on that which is not me. **Fire** comes now upon what you think you know about church or the kingdom…. I AM that I AM is the **All-Consuming Fire** and My kingdom has come with me to unveil the hour of kingdom power that will shower every heart for transformation. Convergence of alignment of hearts. You will become **burning** hearts of kingdom come; Thy will be done…

June 2019:
A fire, a fire, a fire

A sword, a sword, a sword

A sword, a fire; a sword, a fire; a sword, a fire

And people think that I don't care

And people think I'm unaware

But the sword, the **flaming fire**

And [to] those who have turned away

And [to] those who have shut their ears

And [to] those who have shut their eyes

And [to] those who have closed their hearts

I am coming [with a] **flaming sword**…

Oct 2019:
Days like never before.

Days of wonder.

Days of awe.

Days of **fire**.

Days of thunder.

The voice of the Lord thunders from the heavens to the earth and throughout the dimensions.

I am roaring; I am roaring.

My **fire** is roaring across the earth…

February 2020:
The Lord is now releasing a **fire ball of healing**.

October 2020:
Fire, but to stoke the **fire** that the wind of the Spirit might blow and spread His glow. For this is the flow, says the Lord. Heroes will arise in this hour. Mighty soldiers of the Lord will spread the **fire** for that is the Lord's desire to take all of you higher to remove the church from the mire. The headship of the Lord is being restored…

December 2020:
The **chariots of fire** are swarming. I see small **fires** breaking out and the wind of God's spirit them into a **large fire that will burn** across the United States. The land is dry and is primed for an outbreak of My Spirit…

October 2021:
Like a two-edged sword, because there will be more refining; but there will also be periods of great rejoicing. Because of the fruit you will see; oh, oh, there is fruit, there

is fruit coming. There is new fruit coming, refining. Oh, the **fire**, the **refining fire**, oh the **refining fire**. It's coming, big time, less of you individually, and more of Me…

March 8, 2022:

There is **a ring of fire** bubbling up and birthing and bursting forth throughout the Pacific Rim. It is a chain of volcanic eruptions in the Spirit that will soon break forth in the natural. The **fire of God's lava or God's love** is going to pour out upon the people of God that will touch the lost. The Lord is going to pull down the vault and the lost will begin to cry "What must I do to be saved?" The shaking will continue. The Lord will shake everything that does not have the foundation of Christ. Fear will ripple through the nations and humanity will search for answers. But the Lord must first embolden His people. The Lord will extend His lovingkindness to a generation that has not known Him. **Revival fires** will erupt everywhere in Hawaii. It has begun. Have fun in the Son.

November 2022:

I am releasing for this time

Fresh fire, fresh fire, fresh fire

The wind of my Spirit and the breath of my mouth will destroy everything in my way

As I laugh, laugh, laugh at the enemy's design

November 2023:

Fire, fire, fire, fresh fire and a clean anointing of my holy people that must, and is, happening now.

Do not be afraid though, the **fire** must come, and you must walk through it. The **fire** is coming out of the lion's eyes so you must look into the lion's eyes.

Calling to heal the sick. Are you willing to wait in the **fire**?

The **fire** intensifies when we surrender all to Him

Jesus as the son of man

Blue, pink flame of fire above each person

We are all like children, waiting before Him

Time of refreshing, true rest, free from all exhaustion, fatigue, stress

All-consuming fire

Raging fire, lava of His love, the fire is His glory and presence

January 2024:
It is the glory realm. The glory realm **burns with divine fire**... The glory realm is the lava of His love; it is His **burning love** for the lost. The **burning love** for His Bride, the Church... The glory will **burn** away all opposition for the enemy will not come near this realm...

January 2024:
There is a **fire** coming through; there is a purification that is taking place through the eyes. There is a purification that is taken place. The **fire** purifies. I feel a **fire**. I am **burning** so much I perspire. There is a **fire** being released off your tongue. As you speak the **fire** is coming. As you speak the **fire** is going to them because of the **fire** in you. I am feeling the **fire**... **Fire** is consuming... The furnace is here. Prepare ye the way of the Lord. I feel if you want this to happen stand up. Increase the deliverance receive the power. Don't blame me if you start **burning**.

Behold I am coming. I am coming now as a **refiner's fire**. I am coming through every dimension every gate every portal. **My fire will burn** all that has kept you from My power. I must release my power among my people. I must, I must, I must, I must. All dross is **burning** off. You carry

His presence. He is removing the dross so you come forth shining with his glory. I hear the Lord saying it is ok don't be afraid. It is like this has washed over you and cleansed you. He is weeping because the things that have stopped us up. And His power has not been able to flow freely. Let it go. You are safe. Just let it go.

July 21, 2024:
I am the **Fire**, the only **Holy Fire**, the **All-Consuming Fire** that **burns** all that is not of Me away! Yield to **My Fire** and let it consume you, for all that will remain will be only of Me. And all that has enslaved you, from it you will be set free. Melting of deceptions, false hopes and dreams, false identities, false streams of revelation not founded in Me; the **burning** away of all gates and doors of false access points so only that which will remain are my gates and doors through which you may now enter so I can fill you with the more, the more, the more!!

August 2024:
The *fire* of God's desire is on His throne. Discern the cherubim and the discern the wheels and you will be in the vault… The spirit of understanding will manifest to help you get the revelation you need. The light bulb will go on and you catch the **fire** of His desire… The **fire** will fall, and the hearts will **burn** just as the two disciples' hearts **burned** on the road to Emmaus. The sun of righteousness will manifest itself and release **cleansing fire** coupled with **healing fire**…

August 2024:
Turn on the sprinklers, prepare for the **fire**. Call the **fire** department and send the trucks for a **fire** is about to breakout. The embers have been lit, and the wind of the Holy Spirit is blowing. The Father as Power will invade the

hour and the glory will be the beginning of the story. This is the glory realm…

---

[1] A more extensive unedited compilation is available at https://mail.google.com/mail/u/0/#inbox?projector=1&messagePartId=0.1

Appendix Two:
Spiritual Servants of the Most High Who Are on Fire[1]

Ancient of Days (1)

Category: God

History: First discerned, 2009

Definition: Hebrew: *attîq,* 'ancient' (of days), used only in regard to God in Daniel 7[2]

Key Scriptures: Daniel 7:9, 13, 22

Characteristics: Often discerned in the context of being taken into the Ancient of Days court

Angel of the Lord (3)—see also: Angel

Category: Being

History: First discerned, early 2000s, when the furnace appeared

Definition: *NIV Study Bible* note on Genesis 16:8: Since the angel of the Lord speaks for God in the first person (v.10) and Hagar is said to name the Lord who spoke to her: 'You are the God who sees me' (v.13), the angel appears to be both distinguished from the Lord (in that he is called 'messenger'-the Hebrew for 'angel' means messenger') and identified with him. Traditional interpretation has held this 'angel' was a pre-incarnate manifestation of Christ as God's Messenger-Servant. It may be, however, that, as the Lord's personal messenger who represented him and bore his credentials, the angel could speak on behalf of (and so be identified with) the One who sent him. Whether this 'angel' was the second person of the Trinity remains therefore uncertain.

Key Scriptures: Genesis 16:7-13, 18:22-33, 31:11-13, 22:11-18, 32:24-32, 48:15-16 (KJV); Exodus 3:2,4,6-8,14, 13:21-22, 14-19, 32:34 –33:3,14-17; Joshua 5:13-15; Judges 2:1, 6:11-13, 13:1-21; 2 Samuel 24:15-17: 1

Chronicles 21:1, 14:15, 21:18, 24-29; 2 Kings 19:35; Psalm 34; Isaiah 37:36; Zechariah 1:12-13, 3:1-7; Matt 24:44-51, 25:32-42, 26:28, 28:19-20; Luke 4:16-19; John 1:14,18, 9:35-38, 16:1-4, 17:6; Acts 12:21-23; Romans 11:25-26, 15:18-19; Ephesians 1:7; Colossians 2:9; Hebrews 2:14-15,13:5, 9:15; I John 2:1-2; Revelation 5:5, 6:1-17

Characteristics: Located at the Bronze Altar near the entrance to the Tabernacle; may be personal attendant(s) of the Lord (see Genesis 18)

Functions: Revelation; commissioning; deliverance; protection; intercession; advocacy; confirmation of covenant; comfort; judgment; calling to faith and commitment; provision and safekeeping; representative of God's presence; association with glory cloud; heavenly leader of God's army

ARMOR OF LIGHT (6)

Category: God

History:

- On the evening of August 11, 2010, Paul wrote, "Last night at the movie *Salt* in Collingwood, Canada, the power of God fell, and the movie stopped. I got the words, 'His radiant glory' (Hebrews 1:3). The power of God remained on us. Today for the first time I did not feel deliverances while the interns were ministering. I felt His radiant glory the entire time."

- In July 2020, Paul felt a helmet and realized it was the Armor of Light; he could also feel the different pieces of the armor

Definition: Greek: *hopion,* originally any tool or implement for preparing a thing, became used in the plural for 'weapons of warfare'. Once in the NT it is used of actual weapons, John 18:3; elsewhere, metaphorically, of (a) the members of the body as instruments of unrighteousness and as instruments of righteousness, Rom. 6:13; (b) the 'armor' of light, Rom. 13:12; the 'armor' of righteousness, 2 Cor. 6:7; the weapons of the Christian's warfare, 2 Cor. 10:4³ *ho phos,* 'of light'. *Apaugasma,* 'radiant', 'a shining forth' (*apo,* 'from', *auge,* 'brightness'), of a light coming from a luminous body, is said of

Christ in Heb. 1:3, KJV, 'brightness', RV, 'effulgence', i.e., shining forth (a more probable meaning than reflected brightness).[4]

Key Scriptures: Habakkuk 3:4, Romans 13:12 (armor of light), Hebrews 1:3 (radiant glory)

Characteristics: The Lord covers us with His radiant glory

Functions: Protection and a higher level of deliverance power; appear to be connected to thrones

Observations:

- Primarily light is a luminous emanation, probably of force, from certain bodies, which enables the eye to discern form and color. Light requires an organ adapted for its reception (Matthew 6:22). Where the eye is absent, or where it has become impaired from any cause, light is useless. Man, naturally, is incapable of receiving spiritual light inasmuch as he lacks the capacity for spiritual things (1 Corinthians 2:14). Hence believers are called 'sons of light' (Luke 16:8), not merely because they have received a revelation from God, but because in the New Birth they have received the spiritual capacity for it.[5]

- When armor is correctly adjusted, we are rightly connected to Jesus, and indicates how receptive we are

BURNING BUSH / ETERNITY / I AM (25)

Category: God

History: First discerned on July 15, 2016, as the burning bush and knew it was the center of I AM. It became clear on September 30, 2016, that it was I AM as well as eternity when the burning bush showed up at the end of an Academy and was identified as the center of I AM. It was like rotating fire flowing ever inward. El Shaddai was in the center. The bush also seems to be in the center of Mt. Zion and seems to be where the transfiguration was.

Definition: Hebrew: *'ōlam*, 'everlasting', 'eternity';[6] Greek: *aion*, signifies a 'period of indefinite duration'[7]

Key Scriptures: Ecclesiastics 3:11; 2 Peter 3:18

Characteristics:
- Seems to be the location of Mt. Zion
- Exists outside of time
- Connection between heaven and earth
- Located in the heart of God and in the human heart (physical, soul, and spirit)
- Jesus is the door into I AM

Discernment:
- Paul: Bar-like pressure on middle of head from right to left
- Jana: Word of knowledge; sees picture of a horizon; if burning bush, sees horizon, and stepping into it feels like being in the midst of fire; tests this with Hebrew name of God in the midst, 'Elohim Gereb'
- Rob: Feels horizontal bar across top of head
- Larry: Feels encased in a powerful being and have to inquire what is present
- Tobias: Sees golden glory stream, like lines of light streaming out of the Lord; if unrighteous, sees a closed loop, like infinity symbol

CHARIOT(S) OF FIRE (14)

Category: Being

History: First discerned, July 15, 2016

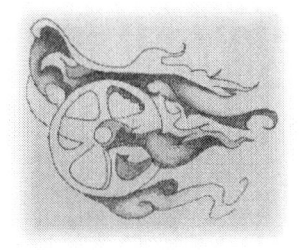

Definition: Hebrew: *kebeb*, 'chariot'; *'esh*, translates as 'fire' 373 times, 'burning' once, 'fiery' once, 'flaming' once, and 'hot' once[8]

Key Scriptures: 2 Kings 2:11, 6:17

Observations:
- Intercession of Melchizedek may stir the fire
- A ministry seems to travel in a chariot
- Seems to rescue DID parts
- Seems to be an association with I AM

CHERUB(IM) (15)

Category: Being

History: First discerned 1992

Definition: Hebrew: *kerub* (ker-oob'), 'cherubim'[9]

Key Scriptures: Genesis 3:24; Exodus 25:17-20, 26:1; 2 Samuel 22:10-11; 1 Kings 6:23-29, 34-35; 1 Chronicles 28:18; 2 Chronicles 3:10-13; Psalm 18:10, 99:1; Isaiah 37:16; Ezekiel 1:4-28, 10:1-22, 28:14-16; 41:17-19; 2 Corinthians 11:14, Revelation 4

Characteristics:
- Living creatures that dwell in the center of the fire in the Cloud of His Presence; Glory of God surrounds them
- Strong wind associated with them
- Look like a man
- Four faces: man, lion, ox, and eagle
- Have four wings (Ezekiel), six wings (Revelation)
- Under wings are two hands of a man
- Each travels straight ahead and does not turn as they move
- Travel as the Spirit travels
- Look like burning coals of fire or torches
- Fire moves back and forth among the creatures
- Burning coals and fire between the wheels
- Lighting flashes out of the fire

- Wheels beside each cherub look like chrysolite. (Strong: a gem, perhaps the topaz; KJV: beryl; NAS: Tarshish stone)
- Wheels appear to intersect each other and do not turn as cherubs move
- Wheels called whirling wheels
- Rims are high and awesome and full of eyes
- An ice expanse over their heads
- Movement of wings sounds like rushing water, voice of the Almighty, the tumult of an army
- Entire body - wings, back, hands, wheels - covered with eyes
- Continually say, "Holy, holy, holy, is the Lord God Almighty who was, and is and is to come."
- Used on Ark of the Covenant and other places throughout the tabernacle/temple

Functions:
- Guardians who carry God's throne; He flies on them
- We may all have personal cherubim and may be moved/transported on them

Observations:
- We do not believe that Lucifer is the cherub mentioned in Ezekiel 28
- Seems to be a connection with thrones

FURNACE (32)—SEE ALSO: ANGEL OF THE LORD

Category: Being

History: First discerned, 2001

Definition: Hebrew: *tannûr*, 'furnace', 'oven';[10] *ṣārap*, 'smelt', 'refine', 'test'[11] and *'esh* (aysh), 'fire',[12] 'refiner's fire'

Key Scriptures: Malachi 3:2, 4:1

Characteristics: A burning fire that results in intense deliverance and purification

Observations:
- A man walked through the furnace during our first tent meeting at the Victorian House in Hesperia and was healed of brain cancer
- A woman who was DID walked through the furnace and was integrated

FIERY STONES (31)

Category: Entity

History: First prophetic words, 2010; first discerned, Sept 21, 2015

Definition: Hebrew: 'esh eben, 'fiery' [AV translates as 'fire' 373 times, 'burning' once, 'fiery' once, 'un-translated variant' once, 'fire + 800' once, 'flaming' once, and 'hot' once; 1 fire; 1A fire, flames; 1B supernatural fire (accompanying theophany); 1C fire (for cooking, roasting, parching); 1D altar-fire; 1E God's anger[13]

Key Scriptures: Ezekiel 28:14,16; Galatians 4:3,9; Colossians 2:8,20

Characteristics: Seem to consist of all components of physical matter, atomic and subatomic particles

Observations: The manifestation of fiery stones is what began Larry Pearson's healing of Crohn's Disease in August 2010.

Discernment:
- Paul: Vibrations on the back of my head
- Jana: Sees them; feels vibration on bottom of feet
- Rob: Burning sensation on right, back of head above neck
- Larry: Strong sense of them under feet and can be standing on them often in the realm; has at times been sensed being dipped in and out of them with a sense of hot and cool
- Tobias: Like updraft of heated air; sees like glowing hot stones, such as used for massage

FLAMING SWORD (22)

Category: Being

History: First discerned March 19, 2020

Definition: Hebrew: *lahat*, 'flame', 'blaze'; *hereb*, 'sword'

Key Scriptures: Genesis 3:24, Psalm 106:16–18

Characteristics: Seems to be used as a weapon of war by the Lord, as well as a limitation on what can be accessed

Observations: The Lord has indicated that those who follow him closely will be able to use the flaming sword

Discernment:
- Paul: Left side of neck next to where gates are discerned
- Rob: Left of where elders are discerned on the bottom of the head

FURNACE (32)—SEE ALSO: ANGEL OF THE LORD

Category: Being

History: First discerned, 2001

Definition: Hebrew: *tannûr*, 'furnace', 'oven';[14] *ṣārap*, 'smelt', 'refine', 'test' [15] and *'esh* (aysh), 'fire',[16] 'refiner's fire'

Key Scriptures: Malachi 3:2, 4:1

Characteristics: A burning fire that results in intense deliverance and purification

Observations:
- A man walked through the furnace during our first tent meeting at the Victorian House in Hesperia and was healed of brain cancer
- A woman who was DID walked through the furnace and was integrated

Discernment:
- Paul: Left top head, (same as Angel of the Lord)

165

- Jana: May see as a square fire; feels heat in front of her
- Rob: Intense fire-like sensation over face
- Larry: Burning in belly and inquire what is present

GLORY OF GOD (38)

Category: Attribute of God

History: First discerned on May 16, 2015, in Ireland; two friends saw two horns they felt were connected to the grid; first discerned the horns on October 22, 2016, while on the North Shore of Oahu and realized it was the Glory of God

Definition: Hebrew: *kabod,* 'glory' [17] Greek: *doxa,* primarily denotes 'an opinion, estimation, repute'; in the NT, always 'good opinion, praise, honor, glory, an appearance commanding respect, magnificence, excellence, manifestation of glory' [18]

Key Scriptures: Exodus 33:18; John 1:14; Habakkuk 3:4

Observations: Glory on Moses' face came from the glory of the letters of the law written on the stone (2 Corinthians 3:7-8)

Discernment:
- Paul: Two streams flowing up on the top back part of my head, like two bolts on the left and right sides; like horns of Moses
- Jana: Feels weight on sides and top of head; feels a vibrating field abound her
- Rob: Two equidistant points on back of head
- Larry: Feel a weighty presence and a deep stillness
- Tobias: Sees as golden, intense radiation

GLORY REALM (41)

Category: Attribute of God, Place

History: First discerned, September 12, 2015

Definition: Hebrew: *kabod,* 'glory'

Key Scriptures: Exodus 24:16, 33:18, Matthew 25:31

Observations: Not only where God is, but relates to God as I AM; healing is felt here

Discernment:

- Paul: Like a waterfall flowing inward on the top of my head
- Jana: Feels an energy field and a heaviness on back of neck
- Rob: Two equidistant points on back of head
- Larry: A powerful expanse below my feet
- Tobias: Feels multiple beings within the realm

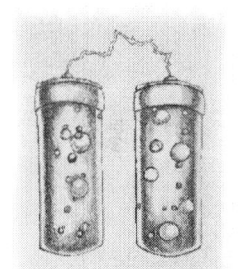

- **GOLDEN PIPES (40)**
- **Category:** Being
- **History:** First discerned October 17, 2014, Kaneohe, Hawaii; a lady had come in for prayer later reported that her hips and her knuckles had been healed; the power of God was very intense.
- **Definition:** Hebrew: $z\bar{a}h\bar{a}b$, gold; $ṣant\bar{e}r\hat{o}t$, pipes
- **Key Scriptures:** Zechariah 4:12, correctly translated as, "Who are these two spikes of the olive trees which are in the hands of the two pressers of gold–the ones who express the gold from (the olives) on them."
- **Functions:** Seem to function as transducers (devices that convert one form of energy (sound, temperature, light etc.) into an electrical signal (voltage, current etc.); we have noticed that when pipes and discerned and functioning, the deliverance intensifies
- **Observations:** Connected to thrones

Discernment:

- Paul: Feels like parallel vertical rods on the back of my head; often an intense burning feeling
- Jana: Sees them
- Rob: Back of head

- Larry: Like Paul, with intense heat
- Tobias: Sees as described; feels like they are boiling

LIGHTNINGS (56)

Category: Entity

History: First discerned around 1994 while in Apple Valley, CA. At that time, I (Paul) did not know what I was feeling, but experienced intervals of pulses as pressure on my head near where I feel angels. The regular pulses at around 90-second intervals lasted for two days, after which the Lord released a strong anointing that caused me to fall to the ground under strong surges of energy. It was not until 2013, that I realized I was feeling lighting strikes.

Definition: Hebrew: *bārāq*, 'lightning', Greek: *astrape*, 'lightning'[19]

Key Scriptures: Psalm 18:14; Revelation 4:5

Observations: Deliverance occurs with lightning strikes

Discernment:
- Paul: Sensation is not sudden, as in earthly lighting, but is a strong pressure that increases and gradually lessens (close to angel's spot)
- Jana: Sees a flash
- Rob: Feels lightning strikes on top, left side of head
- Larry: Sees a flashing presence

RIVER OF GOD (25)

Category: Entity

History: First discerned, March 3, 2017

Definition: Hebrew: *nāhār*, 'river' [20] Greek: *potamos*, 'a river, stream, torrent' [21]

Key Scriptures: Genesis 2:10; Ezekiel 47:5-12; Revelation 21:1-2

Discernment:
- Paul: Feels it flowing across the middle of the head from right to

left
- Jana: Feels a flow around the legs and confirms by feeling with hand

ROOTS (80)

Category: Entity

History: First discerned, 2015

Definition: Hebrew: *sores,* 'root'—used mostly in a figurative sense in the Old Testament. It serves as a natural figure for the lower parts or foundations of something.[22]
Greek: *rhizoo,* 'to cause to take root' is used metaphorically in the passive voice in Eph. 3:17, of being 'rooted' in love[23]

Key Scriptures: Psalm 1; Proverbs 12:3; Colossians 2:7

Characteristics: Seem to be the foundational structure of body, soul and spirit

Discernment:
- Paul: Strong pulling sensation on bottom of feet, often including a cramping sensation in feet
- Jana: Sees roots
- Rob: Underneath feet

MESSENGERS OF FIRE

Who makes His angels spirits, His ministers a flame of fire.
Psalm 104:4

SERAPHIM (85)

Category: Being

History: First discerned, early 2000s

Definition: Hebrew: *saraf,* 'seraph' literally means 'burning one', perhaps suggesting that these creatures had a fiery appearance. Elsewhere in the OT seraph refers to poisonous snakes (Numbers 21:6; Deuteronomy 8:15;

Isaiah 14:29; 30:6). Perhaps they were called burning ones because of their appearance or the effect of their venomous bites, which would cause a victim to burn up with fever. It is possible that the seraphs seen by Isaiah were at least partially serpentine in appearance. Though it might seem strange for a snake-like creature to have wings, two of the texts where seraphs are snakes describe them as 'flying' (Isaiah 14:29; 30:6), perhaps referring to their darting movements.[24]

Key Scriptures: Isaiah 6:1-8

Characteristics: Worship

THRONE OF GOD (27)

Category: Attribute of God

History: First discerned October 1, 2021

Definition: Hebrew: *korsē*, 'throne'

Key Scriptures: Isaiah 6:1; Daniel 7:9; Hebrews 4:16

Characteristics: A fiery throne that sits on wheels

Discernment:

- Paul: Effervescent feeling (senses this is the fire coming up from the feet)
- Jana: Sees thin being; feels fire coming up from feet
- Rob: Feels like burning fire over mouth
- Larry: Left top of head; may sense coals of fire being placed on the mouth

SEVEN SPIRITS OF GOD (86)

Category: Being, entity, place, attribute of God

History: First discerned, 2006; discernment sharpened in 2018

Definition: Identified as the Spirit of the Lord, Spirit of wisdom, Spirit of Understanding, Spirit of Counsel, Spirit of

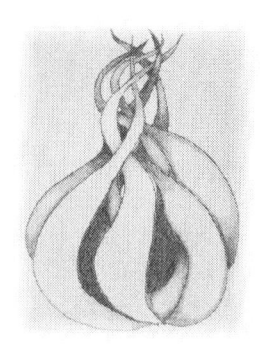

Might, Spirit of Knowledge and Spirit of the Fear of the Lord

Key Scriptures: Isaiah 11:1-2; Zechariah 3:9, 4:10; Revelation 5:6

Characteristics: Located at the candlestick in the tabernacle; also around the throne of God

Functions: Sent out into all the earth

Observations: Tied to the seven eyes of the Lord, which are discerned on the body, and seem to be what those outside of Christianity call chakra points; may appear individually or all at once

Discernment:

- Paul: Sudden increase in temperature that feels like a hot flash (2016); a spot just right of the middle on the left side of the head, at a point in between discernment of left fiery chariots and left pillars (2018)
- Jana: Senses them in a circle and tests by feeling each one with hands
- Rob: Burning sensation on right side of face
- Larry: Burning up the back and inquire what is present

TONGUES (OF MAN) (98)

Category: Being

History: First discerned with hands, 1994; First discerned on head, March 21, 2015

Definition: Greek, *glossa*, (a) 'a language' coupled with *phule*, 'a tribe', *laos*, 'a people', *ethnos*, 'a nation', (b) 'the supernatural gift of speaking in another language without its having been learnt' [25]

Key Scriptures: Psalm 104:4; Acts 2:3; I Corinthians 13:1, 14:2-27; Hebrew 1:7

Characteristics:

- There are tongues that are earthly languages that have not been learned by an individual as well as unique tongues that are angelic languages
- Appears like a flame of fire

Functions: Deliver a message directly from the Lord to an individual

Observations: A tongue of angels is much different than tongues of men in that the tongues is often made up of unusual sounds and tones.

Discernment:

- Paul: Left side of head close to where Holy Spirit is felt and get a hit by saying, "tongue of man" or "tongue of fire"
- Jana: Sees a tongue of fire; word of knowledge
- Larry: Top of head and inquire what is present, knowing in my spirit

TONGUES OF ANGELS (99)—SEE ALSO: TONGUES

Category: Being

History: First discerned March 21, 2015

Definition: Greek: *glossa,* the 'tongues ... like as of fire' which appeared at Pentecost, Greek: *angelos,* 'a messenger' [26]

Key Scriptures: 1 Corinthians 13:1, 14:2-27

Characteristics: Appear as a tongue of fire

Observations: A tongue of angels is much different than tongues of men in that those tongues are often made up of unusual sounds and tones

---

[1] Excerpts taken from *Exploring Heavenly Places: Discernment Encyclopedia for God's Spiritual Creation, Volume 7: Second Edition*

[2] Harris, R. L., Archer, G. L., Jr., & Waltke, B. K. (Eds.). (1999). *Theological Wordbook of the Old Testament* (electronic ed., p. 1056). Chicago: Moody Press.

[3] Vine, Unger & White, p. 37-38.

[4] Ibid., p. 79.

[5] Ibid., p. 369.

[6] Strong.

[7] Vine, Unger, & White, 19.

[8] Strong.

[9] http://biblehub.com/hebrew/3742.htm

[10] Youngblood, R. F. (1999). 2526 תָּנוּר. R. L. Harris, G. L. Archer Jr., & B. K. Waltke (Eds.), *Theological Wordbook of the Old Testament* (electronic ed., p. 974). Chicago: Moody Press.

[11] Hartley, 777.

[12] Strong.

[13] Strong

[14] Youngblood, R. F. (1999). 2526 תָּנוּר. R. L. Harris, G. L. Archer Jr., & B. K. Waltke (Eds.), *Theological Wordbook of the Old Testament* (electronic ed., p. 974). Chicago: Moody Press.

[15] Hartley, 777.

[16] Strong.

[17] Thomas, R. L. (1998). *New American Standard Hebrew-Aramaic and Greek dictionaries : updated edition.* Anaheim: Foundation Publications, Inc.

[18] Vine, Unger, & White, 169.

[19] Vine, Unger & White, Vol. 2, p. 371.

[20] Harris

[21] Vine, Unger & White, Vol. 2, 243.

[22] Austel, 957.

[23] Vine, Unger & White, Vol. 2, 539.

[24] (Biblical Studies Press. (2006). *The NET Bible First Edition Notes* (Is 6:2). Biblical Studies Press}

[25] Ibid., 636.

[26] Ibid., 26.